Joyce Appleby on *Thomas Jefferson*

Louis Auchincloss on *Theodore Roosevelt*

Jean H. Baker on *James Buchanan*

H.W. Brands on *Woodrow Wilson*

Douglas Brinkley on *Gerald R. Ford*

James MacGregor Burns and Susan Dunn on *George Washington*

Robert Dallek on *James Monroe*

John W. Dean on *Warren G. Harding*

John Patrick Diggins on *John Adams*

E. L. Doctorow on *Abraham Lincoln*

Henry F. Graff on *Grover Cleveland*

Hendrik Hertzberg on *Jimmy Carter*

Roy Jenkins on *Franklin Delano Roosevelt*

Zachary Karabell on *Chester A. Arthur*

William E. Leuchtenburg on *Herbert Hoover*

Timothy Naftali on *George Bush*

Kevin Phillips on *William McKinley*

Robert V. Remini on *John Quincy Adams*

John Seigenthaler on *James K. Polk*

Hans L. Trefousse on *Rutherford B. Hayes*

Tom Wicker on *Dwight D. Eisenhower*

Ted Widmer on *Martin Van Buren*

Sean Wilentz on *Andrew Jackson*

Garry Wills on *James Madison*

George Washington

James MacGregor Burns and Susan Dunn

George
Washington

THE AMERICAN PRESIDENTS

ARTHUR M. SCHLESINGER, JR., GENERAL EDITOR

Times Books

HENRY HOLT AND COMPANY, NEW YORK

Times Books
Henry Holt and Company, LLC
Publishers since 1866
115 West 18th Street
New York, New York 10011

LIBRARY OF CONGRESS CATALOGING-IN-PUBLICATION DATA
Burns, James MacGregor.
    George Washington / James MacGregor Burns and Susan Dunn.—1st ed.
    p. cm.—(The American presidents series)
    Includes bibliographical references and index.
    ISBN 0-8050-6936-4
    1. Washington, George, 1732–1799. 2. Presidents—United States—
Biography. 3. United States—History—Revolution, 1775–1783. 4. United
States—Politics and government—1775–1783. 5. United States—Politics
and government—1783–1809. I. Dunn, Susan, 1945– II. Title.
III. American presidents series (Times Books (Firm))
E312.B983 2004
973.3'092—dc22
[B]   2003060758

First Edition 2004

Printed in the United States of America
1   3   5   7   9   10   8   6   4   2

TO

the memory of the first First Lady,

Martha Washington,

AND

the other presidential wives who played their part too

in shaping the American tradition.

Contents

Editor's Note

THE AMERICAN PRESIDENCY

The president is the central player in the American political order. That would seem to contradict the intentions of the Founding Fathers. Remembering the horrid example of the British monarchy, they invented a separation of powers in order, as Justice Brandeis later put it, "to preclude the exercise of arbitrary power." Accordingly, they divided the government into three allegedly equal and coordinate branches—the executive, the legislative, and the judiciary.

But a system based on the tripartite separation of powers has an inherent tendency toward inertia and stalemate. One of the three branches must take the initiative if the system is to move. The executive branch alone is structurally capable of taking that initiative. The Founders must have sensed this when they accepted Alexander Hamilton's proposition in the Seventieth Federalist that "energy in the executive is a leading character in the definition of good government." They thus envisaged a strong president— but within an equally strong system of constitutional accountability. (The term *imperial presidency* arose in the 1970s to describe the situation when the balance between power and accountability is upset in favor of the executive.)

The American system of self-government thus comes to focus in the presidency—"the vital place of action in the system," as Woodrow Wilson put it. Henry Adams, himself the great-grandson and grandson of presidents as well as the most brilliant of American historians, said that the American president "resembles the commander of a ship at sea. He must have a helm to grasp, a course to steer, a port to seek." The men in the White House (thus far only men, alas) in steering their chosen courses have shaped our destiny as a nation.

Biography offers an easy education in American history, rendering the past more human, more vivid, more intimate, more accessible, more connected to ourselves. Biography reminds us that presidents are not supermen. They are human beings too, worrying about decisions, attending to wives and children, juggling balls in the air, and putting on their pants one leg at a time. Indeed, as Emerson contended, "There is properly no history; only biography."

Presidents serve us as inspirations, and they also serve us as warnings. They provide bad examples as well as good. The nation, the Supreme Court has said, has "no right to expect that it will always have wise and humane rulers, sincerely attached to the principles of the Constitution. Wicked men, ambitious of power, with hatred of liberty and contempt of law, may fill the place once occupied by Washington and Lincoln."

The men in the White House express the ideals and the values, the frailties and the flaws of the voters who send them there. It is altogether natural that we should want to know more about the virtues and the vices of the fellows we have elected to govern us. As we know more about them, we will know more about ourselves. The French political philosopher Joseph de Maistre said, "Every nation has the government it deserves."

At the start of the twenty-first century, forty-two men have made it to the oval office. (George W. Bush is counted our forty-third president because Grover Cleveland, who served nonconsecutive terms, is counted twice.) Of the parade of presidents, a dozen or so lead the polls periodically conducted by historians and political scientists. What makes a great president?

Great presidents possess, or are possessed by, a vision of an ideal America. Their passion, as they grasp the helm, is to set the ship of state on the right course toward the port they seek. Great presidents also have a deep psychic connection with the needs, anxieties, dreams of people. "I do not believe," said Wilson, "that any man can lead who does not act . . . under the impulse of a profound sympathy with those whom he leads—a sympathy which is insight—an insight which is of the heart rather than of the intellect."

"All of our great presidents," said Franklin D. Roosevelt, "were leaders of thought at a time when certain ideas in the life of the nation had to be clarified." So Washington incarnated the idea of federal union, Jefferson and Jackson the idea of democracy, Lincoln union and freedom, Cleveland rugged honesty. Theodore Roosevelt and Wilson, said FDR, were both "moral leaders, each in his own way and his own time, who used the presidency as a pulpit."

To succeed, presidents must not only have a port to seek but they must convince Congress and the electorate that it is a port worth seeking. Politics in a democracy is ultimately an educational process, an adventure in persuasion and consent. Every president stands in Theodore Roosevelt's bully pulpit.

The greatest presidents in the scholars' rankings, Washington, Lincoln, and Franklin Roosevelt, were leaders who confronted and overcame the republic's greatest crises. Crisis widens presidential opportunities for bold and imaginative action. But it does not guarantee presidential greatness. The crisis of secession did not spur Buchanan or the crisis of depression spur Hoover to creative leadership. Their inadequacies in the face of crisis allowed Lincoln and the second Roosevelt to show the difference individuals make to history. Still, even in the absence of first-order crisis, forceful and persuasive presidents—Jefferson, Jackson, Theodore Roosevelt, Ronald Reagan—are able to impose their own priorities on the country.

The diverse drama of the presidency offers a fascinating set of tales. Biographies of American presidents constitute a chronicle of wisdom and folly, nobility and pettiness, courage and cunning, forthrightness and deceit, quarrel and consensus. The turmoil perennially swirling around the White House illuminates the heart of the American democracy.

It is the aim of the American Presidents series to present the grand panorama of our chief executives in volumes compact enough for the busy reader, lucid enough for the student, authoritative enough for the scholar. Each volume offers a distillation of character and career. I hope that these lives will give readers some understanding of the pitfalls and potentialities of the presidency and also of the responsibilities of citizenship. Truman's famous sign—"The buck stops here"—tells only half the story. Citizens cannot escape the ultimate responsibility. It is in the voting booth, not on the presidential desk, that the buck finally stops.

—Arthur M. Schlesinger, Jr.

George Washington

Prologue

Slowly the ornate carriage lumbered on its long journey northeastward toward New York. At every stop along the way, outpourings of people crowded around the general, cheering him while church bells rang and cannon boomed. People sang and people wept. Crossing a bridge outside of Philadelphia, he passed under an elaborate arch erected in his honor and was crowned with a wreath of laurels. He rode into Philadelphia on a white horse as twenty thousand citizens struggled to catch a glimpse of their hero. In Trenton women and girls scattered blossoms on the ground before him, singing "Welcome, mighty Chief!"

The little procession—George Washington and two companions—that had left Mount Vernon without ceremony on the morning of April 16, 1789, had turned into a triumphal promenade of republican spirit. A people frustrated by years of war and uncertainty and hardship, a people starved for leadership and direction, citizens denied the power of directly choosing their leaders and often denied any vote at all—these persons were now voting with lungs and legs for their leader, a man on a white horse, a republican hero.[1]

Washington had hoped for a subdued arrival in New York City, where his inauguration would take place. "No reception can be so congenial to my feelings," he had written in late March to the governor of New York, "as a quiet entry devoid of ceremony." But there would be no quiet entry. On the afternoon of April 23, a flotilla of gaily festooned boats of all sizes, their flags waving in the wind, accompanied his barge across Newark Bay toward Manhattan. As one sloop approached the barge, the women on board sang an ode to the general, who lifted his hat in thanks. A Spanish warship fired a salute. Nearing the pier at the foot of Wall Street, Washington could make out masses of people crowded along the waterfront and stretching up the streets behind.[2]

He was emotionally exhausted. "The display of boats, the decorations of the ships, the roar of cannon, and the loud acclamations of the people," he wrote in his diary that evening, "filled my mind with sensations as painful (considering the reverse of this scene, which may be the case after all my labors to do good) as they are pleasing."

Indeed, gloomy thoughts crowded his mind. Neither the elated throngs nor the evidence of his staggering popularity could dissipate his apprehension. He had been the unanimous choice of the Electoral College, but his accession to the chair of government, he had written to a friend in early April, "will be accompanied by feelings not unlike those of a culprit who is going to the place of his execution." Concerned that he possessed neither the skill nor the zeal to manage the helm, he worried that he was placing in jeopardy not only the fate of his countrymen but also his own good name. Still, he was ready to sacrifice his private life and answer the country's call. "Integrity and firmness is all I can promise," he wrote. "These never shall forsake me although I may be deserted by all men."[3]

Was he truly reluctant to accept the nation's highest office? He had made similar noises of diffidence and self-sacrifice when delegates to the Second Continental Congress unanimously chose him to be commander in chief of the revolutionary army in 1775 and again a dozen years later when he had hesitated to attend the

Constitutional Convention. And yet Washington always happened to be in the right place at the right time. A happy set of coincidences? Or a consuming ambition to be at the center of events masked by a virtuoso performance of self-effacement, reserve, and disquiet?

The president-elect had perfected a brilliantly effective formula. By professing his distaste for high office, by reminding people of his yearning for retirement, and by admitting his uncertainty as to his abilities, he had learned to hedge all bets and come out ahead. Even so, there was a note of sincerity in his hesitation to occupy the president's chair. "I have had my day," he had written a few years earlier, painfully conscious of his mortality. And, though ambitious, he did not want to put at risk or injure the reputation he had nurtured for decades. But he also knew that his reputation was not yet fully realized.[4]

The general's revolutionary glory had issued not only from his skill as a military strategist but also from his remarkable farewell in 1783. At the moment of victory, he stunned Americans with his resignation of military power and his even more unusual refusal to seize political power. Instead, he announced his decision to return to his farm. It had been an unprecedented gesture that electrified the world. But relinquishment of power—however unexpected, dramatic, and virtuous—was not enough. The logic and momentum of his career as a fighter for independence and as an advocate for a strong republic called for him to accept one final challenge.

His presidency—his shaping of that office and his consolidation of executive power—would be his ultimate achievement, for it would undergird every future president who would seek to offer strong and determined leadership.

1

Fierce Ambition

"Let your Countenance be pleasant but in Serious Matters Somewhat grave." "Wear not your Cloths, foul, unript or Dusty." "When Another speaks be attentive your Self." "Reprehend not the imperfections of others for that belongs to Parents Masters and Superiours." In 1747, an eager and ambitious George Washington, at the green age of fifteen, was already concentrating on making his way in the world. Meticulously, he copied a list of 110 exacting rules of conduct and civility from the English translation of a French seventeenth-century manual on good manners, the equivalent of a modern self-help book, a kind of How to Be a Gentleman in One Hundred and Ten Easy Lessons. Unlike many other seventeenth-century French maxims, these contained few penetrating psychological insights. But they taught that there was little difference between moral qualities and social ones; they explained that one lived one's life among others, and that, to be successful in society, one must be polite, modest, pleasing, and attentive to others; one must strive to win their confidence and respect. They gave instructions on how to behave with men of greater rank and how to balance deference to the mighty with one's own dignity and ambition.

"Associate yourself with Men of good Quality if you Esteem your own Reputation." "In company of those of Higher Quality than yourself Speak not till you are ask'd a Question." "Strive not with your Superiors in argument, but always Submit your Judgment to others with Modesty." "Contradict not at every turn what others Say." Many of these rules of conduct would serve and steady Washington for the rest of his life—and he would pass on their wisdom to others. "Offer your sentiments with modest diffidence—opinions thus given are listened to with more attention than when delivered in a dictatorial stile," he would write to his nephew in 1787.[1]

The young Washington also turned his attention to men's fashion: he designed a new coat for himself, specifying for the tailor such features as the width of the lapels and the placement of all twelve buttons. "First impressions are generally the most lasting," Washington would write more than forty years later to another nephew, advising the young man that, if he wished "to make any figure *upon the stage*," it was absolutely necessary to "take the first steps right." Washington's letter of advice contained one line on the acquisition of knowledge, one on moral virtues, one on economy and frugality, twelve on choosing well one's friends, and thirty-four on clothing.[2]

Manners and appearance mattered intensely to the adolescent Washington, for his half brother Lawrence had just introduced him to a dazzling, refined, sophisticated world on the Potomac. His eyes lit up when he entered the manor houses of Virginia's upper class, glimpsing the elegant furnishings, hearing the soft-spoken pleasantries of their fashionable inhabitants.

He relished the weeks he was permitted to spend at Lawrence's home, called Mount Vernon, and at Belvoir, the neighboring estate of the Fairfax family into which Lawrence had married. George came to know well Lawrence's brother-in-law, George William Fairfax, and was captivated by his young wife, Sally. The Fairfaxes, like Virginia's other elite, influential families, lived at the pinnacle of Virginia society. Colonel William Fairfax of Belvoir, George William's father, one of the twelve gentlemen who sat on the royal governor's Council of State, was a cousin of Lord Fairfax, peer of the realm, who had been granted title to over 5 million acres of land in Virginia. The colony's political life was transacted on plantations like Belvoir, not in the small towns. In 1760, Virginia had a population of about 173,000 whites and 120,000 slaves, but only a thousand people lived in the capital, Williamsburg, and probably no more than three hundred in Richmond.[3]

Lawrence had become George's mentor and role model. Fourteen years older than George, he had been educated in England and had already served as an officer in an American regiment of the British army, become the adjutant general of the Virginia militia, and won election to the Virginia House of Burgesses.

Their father, Augustine Washington, a speculator in land, was third-generation American, the owner of more than ten thousand acres of Virginia land, fifty slaves, and an iron mine. Still, the Washingtons were not one of the distinguished, powerful families of the day, who might well have owned ten times that amount of land. At Ferry Farm, where Augustine lived in a modest home with his second wife, Mary Ball, and their five children, young George learned reading, writing, and mathematics, occasionally venturing across the Rappahannock River to the raw little town of Fredericksburg. He did not attend college and for the rest of his life would be conscious of what he termed his "defective education."[4]

On April 12, 1743, when George was eleven, his father died. (The following day, less than a hundred miles away, a baby named Thomas Jefferson was born.) Augustine's two sons from his first marriage inherited most of his land. George would inherit, at age twenty-one, Ferry Farm, two thousand acres, three lots in Fredericksburg, and ten slaves. But more important, after his father's death, George visited more often with Lawrence and the Fairfaxes. Decades later Washington would recall times spent at Belvoir as "the happiest moments of my life."[5]

Mount Vernon and Belvoir: magical kingdoms, the gracious

world of Virginia gentlemen-planters, their well-educated, polished sons, their lively daughters. On their estates, they lived "nobly," observed one visitor from France, the Marquis de Chastellux. They dined well; they conversed knowledgeably and interestingly about a wide variety of subjects; they knew and enjoyed the dances of the day. His shrewd intelligence mobilized, George observed them intently. "It is in their power," he wrote to his younger brother, "to be very serviceable upon many occasion's to us, as *young beginner's*."[6]

The price of membership in the small club of Virginia's prestigious families was *land*. Mere money "will melt like Snow before a hot Sun," Washington would later write, explaining that "lands are permanent, rising fast in value." As a teenager, he studied the techniques of surveying—the necessary prelude to the acquisition and development of land—and, in 1748, joined George William Fairfax and others mapping out land in the Shenandoah Valley. Acutely conscious of class distinctions, he looked down upon the poor settlers he encountered there, hating the time he had to spend with a "parcel of Barbarian's." The following year he helped survey lots in the newly established town of Alexandria and was appointed county surveyor in Culpeper County. Paid in cash for his work, he made his first purchases of land. By the age of eighteen he had already bought fifteen hundred acres in Virginia.[7]

And yet not even landed wealth was sufficient for membership in the in-group. There was more. Standing over six feet tall, with his reddish hair, it was hard not to notice Washington, and yet it was *notice*—not just mere visibility but more, that is, the regard and the esteem of others—that he craved most. Success, Washington would emphasize years later to his nephew, depended on how one appeared "in the eyes of *judicious* men." He began the quest for notice by following in his brother Lawrence's footsteps and entering a career in the military: he traveled to Williamsburg, met with the governor, Robert Dinwiddie, and requested a post in the

Virginia militia. George's connection with Colonel Fairfax proved especially helpful. Captivated by the serious, deferential, ambitious young man, Dinwiddie soon complied.[8]

Dinwiddie appointed Major Washington the messenger who would travel into the Ohio country to give an ultimatum to French troops. In the mid-1750s, Britain and France were fighting over control of North America; Versailles had dispatched troops south of Lake Erie to seize control of the vast Ohio country northwest of Virginia. London ordered its Virginia troops to drive the French off "by Force of Arms." It was Washington's mission to find the French position in the wilderness and present the French with a choice: withdraw from the land that Britain claimed or face Virginia troops.

When the French commander rejected the ultimatum, Washington made the arduous trip home and was soon appointed lieutenant colonel in charge of a small force of fewer than two hundred Virginians to confront the French enemy. Although his troops were as untrained in war as he was, he boldly sortied out, in spring 1754, to face a French force of at least a thousand men, aided by large numbers of Indians. Making their way through the thick, trackless forest, led by Indian guides, Washington and his men came upon a small French troop and carried out a surprise attack, only to discover that one of the Frenchmen they killed was an envoy on a mission similar to Washington's earlier one, to warn the British off French land. The shots Washington's men fired marked the start of the French and Indian War.

Washington and his troops proceeded to build a flimsy stockade they called "Fort Necessity." In early July, after indecisive skirmishes, the arrival of fewer reinforcements than he had hoped for, and illness and deep fatigue, Washington and his soldiers were suddenly assaulted in their poorly located fort by nearly a thousand Frenchmen. Washington was resolute in defense, but pinned within the stockade walls, hopelessly overwhelmed, he had little opportunity for generalship. Within hours he lost a third of his troops, dead or wounded. Offered reasonable terms, the young colonel surrendered.

Washington returned to Virginia a defeated man—even more, a bungler who had been at times overly daring and at times indecisive, and who had been unable to enlist Indians to offset the French advantage. He might have had "courage and resolution," General Lord Albemarle, the British ambassador to France, commented, but he simply had "no knowledge or experience in our profession." And yet, miraculously, the twenty-two-year-old soldier was greeted back home by fellow Virginians as something of a hero, if only for his determination and valor under fire. He allowed others to take the burden of blame for the defeat.[9]

After a year's respite from the army, Washington missed the soldier's life and decided once again to join the military, first as a volunteer aide to General Edward Braddock, alongside whom he fought heroically, then, in the fall of 1755—after much negotiation—as commander of the Virginia regiment. To have refused the appointment, he told his mother, who disapproved of his return to military service, would have cast "eternal dishonour" upon him. War between England and France was officially declared in 1756, after which most of the battles would take place farther north. In 1758, Washington's final mission—to seize Fort Duquesne from the French—would end successfully, without a shot. The French had retreated, leaving their fort in flames.[10]

If the whole episode of Washington's five-year military career told something of his limitations, it blazoned forth a crucial aspect of the young colonel in his early twenties—his ever-present ambition.

During his years in the military, Washington had been engaged in two parallel campaigns: one was for military victory, the other was for notice. "The chief part of my happiness," he candidly admitted, was "the esteem and notice" of his country. People could hardly ignore the striking uniforms he had designed and ordered for himself and his troops—blue coats with scarlet and silver cuffs, red waistbands, and hats embellished with silver trim. But the notice he sought required more than cultivated appearance. To win the respect of his social and professional superiors, he would also have to cultivate his own reputation and honor. He longed for evidence that society's leaders held him in higher esteem than the *common run* of provincial officers." Even the official statement of gratitude that he and his troops received from the House of Burgesses in 1754 was not sufficient.[11]

So began his quest for a royal commission in the regular British army, a long journey on horseback to Boston to meet with the acting commander in chief of British forces in America. With an aide and two servants, he left his troops behind and rode off in February 1756, a knight in blue uniform on a quest for his holy grail. Through Maryland and Delaware, across rivers and meadows, to Philadelphia—his first experience of a city and all its diversions. Then on through New Jersey to New York and yet another taste of sophisticated, urban life. Then off to Boston, where a local newspaper reported the arrival of "a gentleman who had deservedly a high reputation for military skill and valor, though success has not always attended his undertakings." The reward for his lengthy voyage and absence of two months? No royal commission was forthcoming. A year later, he went off again on the same errand, now to Philadelphia. Again in vain.[12]

Why the preoccupation—no, the obsession—with rank? Washington himself gave serious thought to this question. Later, as commander in chief of the revolutionary army, he would insightfully explain that whereas the revolutionary forces were fighting for "all that is dear and valuable in Life," the Virginia regiment in the 1750s had been engaged solely in "the usual contest of Empire and Ambition." In those kinds of contests in which fighting men were mere pawns, he remarked, the "conscience of a soldier" had so little at stake that he could "properly insist upon his claims of Rank, and extend his pretentions even to Punctilio." In other words, the ultimate prize of French-English conflict was of so little moral worth, so tangential to the "general Interest" of society, that an officer could rightly be concerned with his own "smaller and partial considerations."[13]

Neither Washington's military campaigns nor his campaign for rank had ended in dazzling success. And yet, by 1758, he was no longer simply a "beginner," as he had written earlier to his brother. He had served as a military leader, been warmly praised by his officers, feted by prominent families in Philadelphia, New York, and Boston. But still no royal commission.

Wouldn't it be less frustrating to return to Mount Vernon, which he had been renting from Lawrence's widow since his death in 1752, marry well, begin his own family, and join the landed gentry and governing class of Virginia? Martha Dandridge Custis, a wealthy young widow, struck Washington as an "agreeable Consort." "Love is too dainty a food to live on *alone*," he would counsel his step-granddaughter years later. The marital partner, he explained to her, should possess good sense, a good disposition, a good reputation, and financial means. To their marriage Martha brought six thousand acres, one hundred slaves, and her two children. For their wedding, Washington ordered his clothes from London. "Would Washington have ever been commander of the revolutionary army or president of the United States, if he had not married the rich widow of Mr. Custis?" asked John Adams, whose own wife was so crucial to his career and happiness.[14]

It was 1759. He was twenty-seven, had just resigned from the military, in which he would not serve again for sixteen years, and had, a few months earlier, won a seat in the Virginia House of Burgesses. Though he had been determined to win the race, he did not solicit votes and, despite the urging of his friends, did not even show his face on Election Day. Still, he spent £40 on his campaign—which consisted mostly of dances, barbecues, and, on Election Day alone, 160 gallons of rum, wine, beer, and punch for the 390 voters. At the first session he attended as a young legislator, the burgesses expressed their official gratitude for "his faithful services to His Majesty and this Colony, and for his brave and steady behavior." Washington rose and bowed, blushing with pleasure.[15]

In the House of Burgesses he mostly listened, intent on absorbing the new protocol of politics. During the ten weeks a year when the burgesses were in session, George and Martha enjoyed the social life in Williamsburg, attending dinner parties and balls. Back home at Mount Vernon, which he inherited in 1761, he worked at making himself indispensable to the community, serving as a vestryman in Truro Parish, trustee of the town of Alexandria, and justice of the county court. With an acute sense of responsibility to others combined with a desire to win their respect, he devoted much of his time to writing letters, settling accounts, acting as executor for the estates of his friends and acquaintances.

His happiest moments were spent at Mount Vernon. His dream was to transform it into a grand English-style manor house and plantation—and, indeed, it soon became a self-sufficient and profitable agricultural and industrial village. In addition to fields of tobacco, wheat, and corn, there was also a dairy, a smokehouse, a cider press, a vineyard, fruit orchards, a flour mill, a sawmill, and a cloth factory. Washington managed and supervised every aspect of his estate, from fishing on the Potomac to the breeding and selling of horses. Indentured white workers toiled along with black slaves. By the mid-1770s, he owned nearly two hundred slaves, coolly exchanging some of them for rum, molasses, and limes. He provided his slaves with little: scant clothing, few blankets, perfunctory medical care. When runaways were caught, they were flogged. But some got away. "God knows I have losses enough in Negroes," he complained. Significantly, the most glaring difference that Washington perceived between blacks and himself—their lack of interest in their reputations—reveals what was most essential and precious to him. "Blacks are capable of much labour," he wrote. "But having . . . no ambition to establish a *good* name, they are too regardless of a *bad* one." In his other business dealings, he watched vigilantly over his profits and did not hesitate to lash out at anyone trying to take advantage of him. "All my concern is that I ever engag'd myself in behalf of so ungrateful and dirty a fellow as you are," he snapped at one associate.[16]

In his manor house, he was served by thirteen house slaves. Clothing, furniture, paintings, dishes, wines, and spices were shipped periodically from London. Busts of famous soldiers— Alexander the Great, Julius Caesar, and others—were ordered, but statues of Bacchus and Flora arrived instead. From England also came a fashionable carriage, adorned with gilded molding and Washington's own crest. He and Martha led an active social life; they entertained often at Mount Vernon and hospitably welcomed their guests.

Fashionable clothing, military busts, and elegant carriages mattered to Washington, but the game was still about land—for investment as well as for prestige. Governor Dinwiddie had promised two hundred thousand acres at the confluence of the Ohio and the Kanawha to the soldiers who fought in the army of 1754, and, when the land was finally distributed years later, Washington secured for himself twenty thousand of the best acreage. Some of the other veterans would protest that he had grabbed the choicest parcels for himself and even swindled them out of their own lots. Washington looked toward western Pennsylvania, too, for land and also sent an agent to scout for land in west Florida. The greatest fortunes and the greatest estates, he noted, were made by "purchasing at very low rates the rich back Lands" that eventually became the most valuable properties. He advised friends to seize the moment—and seize land. Anyone "who neglects the present opportunity of hunting out good Lands," he wrote in 1767, "will never regain it."[17]

Still, it was not all about acquisition, for some of his schemes were visionary: the company he formed to purchase and drain the land called the Dismal Swamp south of the Chesapeake, and his plan for a Potomac canal for shipping and commerce, a waterway that, in his mind's eye, would eventually connect the western territory with the Atlantic states. Navigable inland waterways, he would write after the Revolutionary War, would transport the produce of the western settlers to the Atlantic and increase American exports, while binding those settlers to us "by a chain which never can be broken." "A mind like his," an impressed James Madison would write to Jefferson in 1785 about Washington's extensive plans for inland water transportation, was "capable of great views."[18]

In politics, he was more aggressive about holding on to his seat and shutting out any opponents than he was attentive to the duties of a burgess. Some years he attended no sessions at all. "We missed your friendly services exceedingly," wrote a friend after one of his absences. When he wasn't skipping meetings, it was local issues that concerned him most. One bill he sponsored was meant to protect the purity of local wells by controlling the raising of hogs. But the political landscape was about to shift dramatically.[19]

In 1765, Parliament passed the Stamp Act. His Majesty's government decided to tax all printed materials imported into the colonies—everything from legal documents, insurance policies, and shipping papers to newspapers, almanacs, and even playing cards. It was the first direct tax imposed by Parliament on Americans, and they objected to it furiously. Disturbances and riots swept the colonies. Some men joined underground clubs, called "Sons of Liberty." In Virginia, the stamp agent responsible for collecting the revenues was burned in effigy by a mob and refused to collaborate further with the hated act. Stamp agents across the colonies resigned. Addressing the Virginia House of Burgesses, Patrick Henry proposed radical resolutions, insisting that the right of the colonies to tax themselves was their fortress of freedom. Standing in the doorway a young man overheard his words. Henry "appeared to me to speak as Homer wrote," the twenty-two-year-old Thomas Jefferson said.

But one man remained cool and detached: George Washington. Those who most objected to the Stamp Act, Washington observed, belonged to "the Speculative part of the Colonists," who saw this tax as a "direful attack upon their Liberties." Washington, the landed gentleman, seemed to keep his distance from these speculators—lawyers, shipowners, publishers—suggesting that the act represented an attack on "their" liberties and not on his own. And yet he too considered the act "ill judged" and "unconstitutional," though he believed that economic pressure exerted by the colonies in response to the Stamp Act would be more effective than mere protests and petitions. In the wake of the Stamp Act and other burdensome acts and restrictions on American trade, he believed that Americans should simply import less from England. British merchants, he surmised, "will not be among the last" to wish for a repeal of the Stamp Act. Not only could the colonists easily forgo their luxury imports, they would be motivated to increase their own production of the "necessaries of Life." Britain's repressive actions would ultimately provide "a necessary stimulation to Industry." Indeed, he would soon develop new manufactures at Mount Vernon and discontinue the production and export of tobacco. Washington was thinking as a businessman and budding industrialist, not yet as a revolutionary.[20]

The unpopular Stamp Act was repealed, but two years later England passed the Townshend Acts, imposing duties on paints, glass, paper, and tea. The Virginia House of Burgesses, with remarkable unanimity, demanded the repeal of the acts and the return to the "full enjoyment of all our natural and constitutional rights and privileges." Washington, attending to his various business interests, was absent during the debate. Not until the spring of 1769 did he take a public position against British policies. His ideas had evolved, and now, decidedly less sanguine than he had been, he felt the urgency of defending "the liberty which we have derived from our Ancestors" against "our lordly Masters in Great Britain." But how?[21]

The cities of Boston, New York, and Philadelphia had joined in a boycott of British exports. Washington and his friend George Mason agreed that it was crucial for Virginians as well to curtail importation of British goods. The little comforts of life, George Mason wrote to Washington in April 1769, meant nothing "in competition with our Liberty." A boycott of British products, the pragmatic Washington replied, would also help eliminate Virginians' oppressive debts to merchants in England and lessen their financial distress. But if a few "selfish designing men" and some "clashing interests" should prevail and a uniform nonimportation agreement not go into effect, might the situation come to violence? Washington refused to rule out the possibility of a military confrontation. No man should "hesitate a moment" to use arms, he wrote, but, he added, force "should be the last resource." Two years earlier, an inflamed Patrick Henry had cried out in the House of Burgesses, in a thinly disguised warning to George III, that Caesar had had his Brutus; now Washington joined the few who, before the 1770s, had already begun to contemplate armed conflict with England.[22]

At their May 1769 session, the burgesses issued "an humble, dutiful, and loyal address" to the king, "praying the royal interposition in favor of the violated rights of America." Irate, the governor imperiously dissolved the assembly. The burgesses withdrew en masse to the Raleigh Tavern—the Williamsburg equivalent of the French "Tennis Court"?—where they spoke heatedly of their determination to defend the colony's liberties. Then Washington addressed them, presenting the nonimportation plan he and Mason had drafted. The plan was accepted. Virginians would join other Americans in importing fewer luxury items from England. Whereas they used to enjoy indulging in European fashion, Benjamin Franklin remarked, Americans' pride now lay in wearing *their old clothes* over again, till they can make new ones." For his part, Washington stated that he would "religiously adhere" to the list of prohibited imports, adding that he would have wished "it to be ten times as strict." But the agreement soon faltered, and Washington resumed ordering clothing and furniture from England.[23]

And yet, when he had his portrait painted by Charles Willson Peale in 1772, he would unpack his old clothes and pose for the artist in the blue uniform of the Virginia regiment that he had not worn in more than thirteen years. Was he unwilling to appear in fashionable, imported apparel? Or might a calculating Washington have sensed that conflict was in the air and decided to remind his fellow Americans of his military experience? With a musket behind him, his sword at his side, a thoughtful expression on his face, he posed confidently for Peale. It would be the artist's task, Washington wrote, to describe "to the World what manner of man I am."[24]

What manner of man was he in 1772, at the age of forty? A brave, disciplined, tenacious military leader who had met with more failure than success; an acquisitive planter, harsh slave owner, and profit-oriented businessman; a politician who for years had been more interested in local roads and hogs than international affairs; an ambitious, self-made man hungry for notice; a class-conscious member of the gentry who enjoyed dancing, cards, and fox hunting. Would this man, who had been principally concerned with his own self-interest and advancement, be able to bring intellectual depth and gravitas along with a profound commitment of mind and heart, one that he had not yet demonstrated, to the astonishingly daring and complex task of leading an infant nation in a war for independence against the mightiest power on the face of the planet? Could this elitist southerner with aristocratic inclinations fathom and embody the hopes of revolutionary Americans and of reformers around the world? Not all those who admired and respected him would have dreamed that he could.

2

The Education of a Soldier

Tea. So insignificant. And yet these slight, dried leaves and a paltry threepence tax, the English politician Edmund Burke remarked in April 1774, were shaking the pillars of a commercial empire that encircled the globe. For his part, George Washington experienced the English tax on tea in personal, even physical terms, as an invasion of his very person. "I think the Parliament of Great Britain," he wrote, "hath no more right to put their hands into my pocket, without my consent, than I have to put my hands into yours for money." Freedom for Washington and other Americans was not an abstract philosophical concept: it simply signified power over the granting of their own money.[1]

In December 1773, to protest the new Tea Act that reminded Americans of the still-standing tax on tea (and which also gave the East India Company a monopoly on exporting tea to America and choosing a select group of colonial merchants to sell the tea), a few dozen men, disguised as Indians, boarded three ships in Boston harbor and dumped hundreds of crates of tea overboard. It was the Boston Tea Party. The destruction of the tea was a move "so bold, so daring, so firm, intrepid, and inflexible," wrote John Adams, that it was sure to have major historical consequences. Tea was the drug of the tyrant, people shouted. In London, bills that would be known as the Coercive Acts were passed by Parliament, closing the port of Boston until that city provided restitution and imposing other political restrictions on Bay Staters.

But colony-wide solidarity was now growing. Hundreds of miles from New England, Virginians realized that the shutting down of commercial shipping trade in Boston would have devastating effects on that city's economy and that other American ports were also vulnerable. In Williamsburg, the burgesses agreed that the day the port of Boston was to be closed would be a day of fasting. Virginians would pray to God to give them "one heart and one mind firmly to oppose, by all just and proper means, every injury to American rights." Two days later, the angry governor, Lord Dunmore, once again dissolved the House of Burgesses. But the burgesses met anyway in the Raleigh Tavern, as they had in 1769. There they declared that "an attack, made on one of our sister colonies, to compel submission to arbitrary taxes," would be considered an attack on all of British America. They proposed an annual congress of delegates from all the colonies to deliberate on matters concerning the "united interests of America."[2]

Washington was chafing at the bit. Though he had criticized the tea party in Boston, his thinking had evolved; now he was not only outraged by the infringement on American freedom but also impatient with his fellow Virginians. It was pointless, he felt, to "whine and cry for relief" or to send still more "humble and dutiful" petitions to the throne. Had Parliament even deigned to look at those already sent? The people of Boston had been "abused, grossly abused," he said, by an arbitrary power bent on violating "the most essential and valuable rights of mankind." Would Americans do nothing but "supinely sit and see one province after another fall a prey to despotism?" Instead of protecting the people in their colonies, Washington fumed, London was endeavoring "by every piece of Art and despotism to fix the Shackles of Slavery upon us."[3]

Slavery: the most deplorable form of human degradation and abjection conceivable, even to slave-owning Americans. The vast multitude of slaves on Virginia soil, commented Edmund Burke in a speech to Parliament on conciliation with America, made Virginians even more jealous of their freedom than other Americans. Freedom for men like Washington, Burke hypothesized, was not merely an enjoyment, but "a kind of rank and privilege." As if confirming that analysis, Washington and his friends repeatedly described their struggle with England as resistance against enslavement, displaying a kind of sophisticated indifference to their own collaboration in black slavery. Americans had to assert their rights, he maintained in 1774, or they would become, over time, "tame and abject slaves as the blacks we rule over with such arbitrary sway." The following year, he again remarked that "the once happy and peaceful plains of America are either to be drenched with Blood, or Inhabited by Slaves. Sad alternative."[4]

No, there would be no concessions to bondage: Americans stood ready to organize, to use economic sanctions, and, if necessary, to fight. It was no longer simply a question of the economic self-interest of certain upper-class planters. Larger issues were at stake, and Washington became convinced that "the voice of *mankind*" was with him. Indeed, he and his friends perceived that Americans were engaged in something more significant than a provincial struggle against taxes: it would be a radical battle for the liberation of "mankind." Washington confessed that he would have preferred that the dispute be left to future generations to contend with, but since the crisis had arrived, he and other Americans would meet it head-on. A "shock of electricity," commented Thomas Jefferson, bolted through the air on the August day in 1774 when delegates to a special session of the Virginia assembly chose Washington, Peyton Randolph, Patrick Henry, and others to represent them at the First Continental Congress. There, despite the colonies' cultural, political, and economic differences, delegates would focus on their common interests and defense.[5]

• • •

Dirty, dusty, and fatigued, the fifty-six delegates to the First Continental Congress streamed into Philadelphia in September 1774,
many meeting one another for the first time. Washington, one
delegate noted, had an "easy, soldier like air and gesture." John
Adams looked forward to meeting him, for he had heard that the
planter from Mount Vernon was an eloquent speaker. The gentlemen from Virginia, Adams noted in his diary, "were the most spir-
ited" of all the delegates in Philadelphia. Indeed, next to the
Virginians, commented one Pennsylvanian, "the Bostonians are
mere Milksops."[6]

In the taverns and elegant homes of Philadelphia, the delegates drank, dined, and socialized. What did they talk about?
Consensual social contracts, constitutions, self-government, the
independence of the colonies. The man who had always been self-
conscious about his defective education was now receiving the
education of a revolutionary. "Much abler heads than my own,"
Washington wrote, were instructing—and convincing—him on
questions of rights, laws, and constitutions. He, too, would soon be
a thinking revolutionary, writing about arbitrary power and viola-
tions of the "sacred compacts of government." In Philadelphia he
spoke "very modestly," Silas Deane of Connecticut noted, but in a
"determined style and accent."[7]

The delegates got quickly to work, supporting resolutions that
denounced British repression in Boston as well as the suspension
of colonial assemblies and the presence of British troops in America. They agreed to a boycott of British imports and reaffirmed the
rights of the colonists to life, liberty, and property. They would take
nothing but defensive actions and yet they pointedly stated that
they would not act contrary to "the principle of self-preservation."
The resolutions of the First Continental Congress succeeded in
balancing a promise of restraint and a threat of force, historian
Jack Rakove remarked. Moreover, the delegates proved that they
could deliberate and act collectively. What did they *not* do? They
did not agree to provide restitution for the tea dumped in Boston

harbor, and—more radically—they did not recognize the right of Parliament to regulate the affairs of the colonies. The Congress had become the de facto government in America. His own authority in Virginia, Governor Dunmore reported, was now "entirely disregarded if not wholly overturned."[8]

The session of Congress over, the men returned home. That winter, while the king continued to speak belligerently about the resistance and disobedience in Massachusetts, Washington sensed that the situation was coming to a head and agreed to drill army volunteers. In March 1775, representatives from Virginia's counties met to choose delegates to the Second Continental Congress, and once again they elected Washington, Peyton Randolph, Patrick Henry, and others. They also voted to prepare their colony to defend itself, heeding Henry's stirring call, "We must fight! Give me liberty or give me death!" Especially after the clash of British troops and American volunteers at Lexington and Concord in April, Americans indeed were experiencing new feelings of militant patriotism. "It is my full intention," Washington wrote to his brother Jack that month, "to devote my Life and Fortune in the cause we are engaged in, if need be."[9]

"Colonel Washington appears at Congress in his uniform," noted John Adams, "and by his great experience and abilities in military matters, is of much service to us." In May 1775, Washington had taken to Philadelphia the old blue military uniform he had worn only once—for Peale's portrait—since the French and Indian War. Was it a calculated gesture? Always attentive to the importance of costume, did he wish to communicate a message of military experience and readiness? Neither an intellectual like John Adams nor an orator like Patrick Henry, Washington could offer the unique combination of his past military service, wealth, integrity, and good judgment. Even though he had not excelled during his years in uniform, he had come to understand logistics, strategy, discipline, and leadership. An aggressive, courageous man, he was, as he once said, "bent to arms."[10]

The situation in the country was dangerous and critical, the Congress declared, and delegates voted that all the colonies be put immediately into a state of defense. In a fateful step, Congress then declared that the volunteer soldiers in Boston would form a new Continental Army, to which six companies of riflemen would be added, and it authorized salaries for the soldiers.

But who would lead that army? John Adams proposed George Washington. It was a brilliant suggestion: a Virginian commander in chief leading Massachusetts volunteers would immediately transform the army into a truly national force. Even before the colonies declared war or independence, even before they constituted a nation, they would have in Washington a national leader. "He seems discrete and virtuous," wrote another New Englander at the time, "no harum-scarum, ranting swearing fellow, but sober, steady, and calm." While delegates debated his nomination, Washington quietly absented himself. Finally, his unanimous selection as commander in chief was announced. "The liberties of America depend upon him," wrote John Adams to his wife two days later.[11]

Washington had achieved what he had always desired: center stage in the life of his country. Notice and esteem were his. He thanked the members of the Continental Congress for the high honor they had bestowed upon him and promised to exert all the power he possessed "for the Support of the glorious Cause." And yet he also expressed more than a little ambivalence about his new role. Aware of the vicissitudes of Fortuna and the role of luck in leadership and conscious as ever of the importance of his reputation to him, he commented that "lest some unlucky event should happen unfavourable to my reputation, I beg it may be remembered by every Gentleman in the room, that I this day declare with the utmost sincerity, I do not think my self equal to the Command I am honoured with." In his conclusion, he refused all compensation, except for his own expenses, explaining that he had not accepted this position for any "pecuniary considerations." His words communicated gravitas and modesty: he portrayed himself in public as humbled by power, wary of its awesome responsibilities.

A few days later, in a letter to his wife, Martha, he informed her that he had accepted the command of the Continental Army—reluctantly. "It was utterly out of my power to refuse this appointment," he wrote, "without exposing my character to such censures as would have reflected dishonor on myself and given pain to my friends." Then, in a warmer note, he confessed that he would enjoy "more real happiness and felicity" at home with her for one month than on the world stage for fifty years. Yet, he mused, "a kind of destiny" to which he could only accede had imposed this high position and burden on him. The following month, writing to a fellow officer, he repeated his message that "sacrifice" for one's country bestowed on a man more "real Honor than the most distinguished Victory." From now on, he promised, he would devote himself solely to "American Union and Patriotism." All smaller and partial considerations would "give way to the great and general Interest."[12]

Now his self-portrait was complete: he had added key themes of character, self-sacrifice, destiny. This was the public persona that Washington deliberately forged for himself and that would serve him for the rest of his political life: a man fully conscious of his own limitations, dedicated to public service, gravely willing to sacrifice himself for his country, proud of his symbolic role embodying American nationhood and unity. None other than John Adams quickly confirmed and spread this public image of Washington: the new commander in chief was a "gentleman of one of the first fortunes upon the continent," Adams enthusiastically wrote, "leaving his delicious retirement, his family and friends, sacrificing his ease, and hazarding all in the cause of his country!" What neither Adams nor the public perceived was a ferociously ambitious man, managing to overcome his insecurities and apprehensions, wearing the self-effacing mask of modesty, a man fiercely protective of his own reputation. Washington hardly needed the talent of Charles Willson Peale to describe to the world "what manner of man" he was. Skillfully and purposefully, he painted his portrait himself.

That summer, a prescient Edmund Burke exhorted his fellow members of Parliament to "keep the poor, giddy, thoughtless people of our country from plunging headlong into this impious war." He spoke for two and a half hours, only to see Parliament reject his proposals for conciliation with America by a vote of 270 to 78.

The defeats and victories of the Revolutionary War have long been etched in the American memory: the British forays into Lexington and Concord, harassed by the "minute men" alerted by the "midnight ride of Paul Revere"; the battle of Bunker Hill, won by the British but a moral victory for the tenacious Americans; Benedict Arnold's successes in the northern reaches of the Hudson River; Washington's assuming command of the Continental Army, seventeen thousand strong in the Boston area; the moves of both American and British forces to the New York region, where General Sir William Howe scattered the continental troops in battles ranging from Brooklyn Heights to Manhattan; Washington's skillful retreat into New Jersey, marred by a humiliating defeat in White Plains; the Americans' surprise victories at Trenton and Princeton, followed by Howe's occupation of Philadelphia in the fall of 1777 and the American retreat into the cold winter of Valley Forge. By now the war had assumed continental dimensions— with victories and defeats north and south as well as in the mid-Atlantic states—and indeed global proportions with the outbreak of war between France and Britain in July 1778.

While the American forces slowly extended their territorial control despite bitter defeats, the war as a whole approached military stalemate and a crisis of morale among the Americans: mutinies broke out in Pennsylvania and New Jersey, and Washington suffered the desertion of Arnold. But the tide of battle eventually shifted with the landing of French troops in Yorktown in 1781. Cornwallis's dramatic surrender to Washington soon followed. Though hostilities would continue for a few more months, the war was effectively over. "An American Planter," Benjamin Franklin would write to an English friend in 1784, "was chosen by us to Command our Troops, and continued during the whole War. This Man sent home to you, one after another, five of your best Generals baffled, their heads bare of Laurels, disgraced even in the Opinion of their Employers." Still, the laurel-covered Washington, in the end, had needed the intervention of the French.

Even so, Franklin's "American Planter" had become a remarkable military leader. After mishandling the defense of New York, he met a series of victories and defeats, but he always learned from experience. Setbacks seemed to steel him as he led a highly diverse set of army generals, including imported notables like the Prussian Baron von Steuben, and later his French protégé, the Marquis de Lafayette, sometimes doing more mediating than commanding. He kept his army together amid the privations of Valley Forge. He could be hard on his subordinates, sometimes aggressively moving to check "those officers who possessed the power to constitute a potential threat to his position," as historian John Ferling noted. But Washington matured along with his generals, and he gave them a lesson in the most crucial qualities needed in the agonizingly long war—tenacious persistence and absolute determination, until the war was won.

During the war, the onetime parochial Virginian became a national leader—even a continental leader, to the extent that he had to deal with problems arising beyond the boundaries of the thirteen states themselves. The war actually consisted of hundreds of battles and local skirmishes, up and down the Eastern Seaboard from Maine to the Gulf Coast, as the British fleets sacked vulnerable ports and their infantry sortied into the interior. Washington had to tend to his "Western flank," where the British often attacked with the help of Indian tribes. He had to move his military headquarters from Boston to New York to New Jersey to Pennsylvania. Inevitably, he came to know officers from the whole country—their state loyalties, regional biases—and he had to forge them into a national army.

During the war, the onetime Virginia backbencher became a skillful—albeit informal—political leader, especially in his relationship with the Continental Congress. He appeared before the entire Congress and also met on occasion with its committees. His merit, prestige, and personality were usually enough to gain cooperation from the delegates, and, though he could not always depend on their support, he invariably treated them with respect and deferred to their authority, establishing the crucial principle of the subordination of the military to the nation's political leaders. And he had to learn the art of transactional leadership, too, as he dealt with state politicians, local interests, and—most tiringly— with applications for the officer corps sponsored by congressional and state politicos.

As military and political leader, Washington also had a shrewd awareness of the importance of his public image, for it was he alone, in his multifaceted role, who incarnated the new nation. He rarely if ever refused to sit for an artist who desired to paint his portrait. With a growing understanding of the complex interplay between leaders and followers, he grasped that, to defuse an incipient rebellion among his officers, a few personal words and an eloquent gesture were more effective than stern admonitions. At the end of his words to the would-be rebels, he seemed to falter. "Gentlemen," he said, "you will permit me to put on my spectacles, for I have not only grown gray, but almost blind, in the service of my country." His self-effacing words, his reminder of his own sacrifice, left the officers in tears.

And finally, during the war, Washington became a revolutionary leader. In truth, he was the commander in chief of a war for independence against the British, not the head of the kind of radical, tumultuous social and political upheaval that would later transform and overwhelm France during his presidential years. But in the context of the revolution America experienced, he was among its most passionate proponents, pushing his countrymen—many of whom, he noted, felt a "steady Attachment" to royalty—toward the radical idea of an independent republic, even seeking to reward the firebrand Thomas Paine for writing *Common Sense,* a book that, he said, had worked "a powerful change in the Minds of many Men." Still, although Washington was a republican, he was no democrat. Certainly he was not the kind of general to consort or commune with his corporals and privates. On the contrary, the army in Massachusetts, he confided to his friends, was composed of "an exceeding dirty & nasty people," and the degree of "familiarity between the Officers and Men" he found in New England appalled him. And yet he could not have succeeded in mobilizing his troops, steering them in battle, and articulating their goals without responding in some degree to the social and economic aspirations of these men and the people who supported them.[13]

All these qualities—military skill and judgment, national and continental vision, political astuteness, and revolutionary leadership—would undergird the strength of his later presidency: executive command, national and continental purpose, legislative partnership, and—to some degree—popular leadership.

But at the end of the war in November 1783, Washington seemed to have no thoughts of continuing in public life. Bidding farewell to the armies of the United States, he thanked the men—"a patriotic band of Brothers"—for playing a part in the "wonderful revolution" that had taken place. The "enlarged prospects of happiness" that had been created and confirmed by American independence, he said, "almost exceeds the power of description." Two months later, he announced to Congress his intention to retire from the "great theatre of Action" and take his leave "of all the enjoyments of public life." Congressmen and spectators all wept, reported Washington's military aide James McHenry that same day. The general's hand trembled as he read from his speech, his voice faltered, McHenry continued, "and the whole house felt his agitations." The general would not cling to power; he would not cast himself as monarch.

Around the world, people were astonished by this self-effacing general. The ultimate reward Washington had always sought was an honorable reputation and the esteem of his peers. His willingness to resign from his position of power only burnished his image. The Virginian, like the victorious Roman soldier Cincinnatus, went home to his plow.

3

"Radical Cures"

"For God's sake, tell me what is the cause of all these commotions," wrote Washington to a friend in the fall of 1786. The alarming news of disturbances in western Massachusetts had come crashing in on the serene surroundings of Mount Vernon. The former commander in chief seemed to be living peacefully though busily in Virginia, hatching ways to improve and extend navigation on the Potomac and James Rivers, redesigning his manor house, importing exotic animals, supervising the sowing of seeds, the stacking of hay, and the laying out of roads and serpentine walks, riding around his property, exploring his outlying plantations and parcels of land. As he entertained a steady stream of invited and uninvited visitors, he luxuriated in the order and beauty of his estate, with its formal gardens, greenhouses, deer park, and graceful drives.

But the life of a wealthy planter was not carefree. "Most of my transplanted trees have a sickly look," he wrote in his diary in May 1785. Not a single ash tree had unfolded its buds, the lime trees were withering, the hemlock was almost dead, the honeysuckle was only half alive.[1]

Nor was the life of a civic-minded American carefree. Washington was deeply concerned about the state of the confederation.

"Retired as I am from the world," he wrote to John Jay in the summer of 1786, "I frankly acknowledge I cannot feel myself an unconcerned spectator." Indeed, he was spending much of his time commenting, with growing intensity and disquiet, on political affairs. His first reaction to events in the North was sheer incredulity.[2]

In the small villages of the Berkshires, hundreds of rough-hewn men, crushed by debt, had flocked to join Daniel Shays's rebellion. They were protesting the confiscation of their property— their farms and their cattle—for unpaid debts, and the jailing of some debtors. Times were hard in Massachusetts after the Revolutionary War; the economy was in recession, and the state legislature had imposed heavy taxes to pay for war debts. "If you Dont lower the taxes we'll pull down the town house about you ears," wrote one man to the governor. "We country men will not be imposed on. We fought of our Liberty as well as you did." Inflamed by the loss of the precious right to own property, the rebels' tactic was to occupy the local courthouses and free prisoners. False rumors that Shays had an army of twelve thousand spread like wildfire. In Boston, panicked politicians overreacted, shouting treason and raising an army to crush the revolt. "We are now in a State of anarchy and confusion, bordering on a Civil War," one Bostonian wrote.[3]

Washington cut to the heart of the matter. If the rebels had real grievances, they should be acknowledged and addressed, he wrote. Otherwise the full force of the government should be employed against them. He wanted fair government—but strong government.

While the insurgents felt cheated of their rights and property, men of Washington's class feared for the survival of the nation. It was a question of *order*. "It is but the other day," Washington remarked, "that we were shedding our blood to obtain the . . . Constitutions of our own choice and making; and now we are unsheathing the sword to overturn them." If government could not check these disorders, he wondered, what security had Americans for life, liberty, or property?[4]

Up and down the Berkshire countryside ranged the Massachusetts state militia, routing the rebels. Hundreds escaped into New York and Vermont; thirty were killed or wounded. The victory of the forces of order was small consolation to Washington. Repression was not the answer. Nor was it the decision in Boston to disenfranchise the rebels and deprive them of their political rights. Not only might that backfire, he remarked to Madison, giving "birth to new instead of destroying the old leaven," but the real underlying problem had not been addressed. "A thorough reform of the present system," he wrote to his fellow Virginian, "is indispensable."[5]

In his mind's eye, Washington saw the young nation tottering at "the brink of a precipice." Little was going right. Under the weak Articles of Confederation, the states had the power to regulate commerce and impose taxes. The confederation's Congress—there was no executive, only committees with ever-changing membership—was charged with diplomatic relations and coining and borrowing money. And yet the government seemed incapable of conducting foreign and economic policy. England was restricting American commerce by closing her ports to American shipping, and she still had military posts inside America's northern borders. While many businesses were failing, the states could not agree on how to regulate commerce and impose retaliatory measures. Worse, Spain had closed the Mississippi to American navigation as well. The dominance of local state interests and the rise of populist movements were adding to the fragility and instability of the national government.[6]

Already during the war Washington had been dismayed by the problems in chains of command no less than chains of supply. Indeed, the reason why the war had dragged on for so long and the cost of victory had been so great, he explained to a friend, was a "want of energy in the Federal Constitution." State governments could not even be counted on to support the one overriding goal of winning the war. "How strange it is," he had observed, "that Men, engaged in the same Important Service, should be eternally bickering, instead of giving mutual aid!" Preoccupied almost entirely with their own local concerns, the states had even taken it upon themselves, he wrote, to decide whether or not they would comply with orders of Congress, in what manner they would comply, and at what time! The multiplicity of state governments resembled "a many headed Monster" unable to keep on track. As for the members of Congress, when they were not lost in slumber, they were meandering through the states, migrating from Philadelphia to Princeton to Annapolis to Trenton and then to New York. How could independence be achieved, Washington asked in 1778, unless Americans believed that they constituted one people with one sense of purpose and one overriding goal?[7]

Upon resigning as commander in chief in 1783, Washington had spoken to his troops with utter confidence about the future. But to the state governors he was more candid. Fatal consequences would ensue unless the states agreed to a "Supreme Power to regulate and govern the *general concerns*" of the union. Short of that, he said bluntly, the nation was on "political probation."[8]

Washington was a man of parts: not only a soldier, a general, a planter, an entrepreneur, a pragmatist, an idealist, he was also an astute political thinker who had made an accurate diagnosis of America's political ills and would offer a potent prescription for the kind of government needed by the faltering confederation—if the country was to achieve the future greatness he foresaw. What kinds of institutions were required? It would be the climax of "absurdity and madness," he judged in 1786, not to have a strong Congress, "with ample authorities for national purposes." But even more important was an effective executive: the Articles of Confederation had allowed for only a feeble executive committee that was part of Congress. The reins of government, Washington emphasized, should be "braced and held with a steady hand."

Over and over he pounded home his message: the most critical ingredient in government was energy. Only by lodging somewhere a power that would pervade the whole union in an "energetic manner" could the nation survive.[9]

But he was not optimistic. Though after the war he had assured his friends in Europe that the foundation of a "great Empire" had been laid, he minced no words with his American friends. "Our federal Government is a name without substance," he wrote late in 1784. Half-starved and limping, it appeared to be "moving upon crutches, and tottering at every step." The following year he had given up on the idea of granting Congress more power, for congressmen, afraid to exert any authority, lost no opportunity to hand power back to the states. Why, even respectable citizens, hungry for strong government, he remarked in 1786, had begun "without horror" to entertain the idea of establishing a monarchy in America. By early 1787, he could not skirt the conclusion that the nation was heading toward "some awful crisis."[10]

Tinkering with the Articles of Confederation no longer seemed a reasonable or realistic alternative. Several times, in the early 1780s, there had been attempts to modify them and strengthen the power of Congress. But many Americans remained mistrustful of centralized, national political authority, and all efforts at reform had come to naught. Perhaps the stalemate was fortunate, since the most realistic scenario on the horizon in 1787, for some American leaders like Benjamin Rush and James Madison who favored a strong central government, appeared to be a full-blown constitutional convention, a radical reconceptualization of the fundamental political contract.[11]

The convention was scheduled to take place in Philadelphia during the summer of 1787. But would the general agree to attend? Probably not. Though he favored the convention and wished to see "any thing and every thing essayed," he nevertheless worried that the experiment might fail, for the states were "not likely to agree" on any plan for a new national government. That failure would place "a person in my situation," he confided to a friend in 1786, in a particularly "disagreeable predicament." Indeed, his reputation had grown but so had his attention to its luster. Even Madison fretted that Washington's great prestige might suffer if he were to participate in any "abortive undertaking."[12]

Complicating matters, Washington had declared in 1783 his intention to retire from public life. Wouldn't such backtracking harm his reputation? he asked. Or, on the contrary, would a refusal to go to the convention be viewed as "dereliction to republicanism," diminishing his standing in the eyes of his peers?[13]

A few months before the meeting in Philadelphia was to begin, Washington informed a friend that his "first wish" was "to do for the best, and to act with propriety." But what course should he follow? Would that friend inform him, confidentially, what the public expected of him, "that is, whether I will, or ought to be there?" The consensus of all those whose advice he sought was that he should go. Indeed, the indispensable man proved that he was an expert stage manager, having skillfully incited the pressure on himself to attend the convention. He anticipated that to get Cincinnatus to Philadelphia, others would have to drag him from his plow. Carefully weighing his obligations and his self-interest, the general finally decided to join the other delegates. "The pressure of the public voice was so loud," he wrote to Lafayette, that he could not resist. In light of his own outspoken pronouncements about the importance of a strong executive, now no one could accuse him of trying to grab power in Philadelphia. But what would he have decided, we may wonder, had he not been so concerned with his reputation? And we may also wonder whether his decision to attend the convention and return to public life was as "utterly repugnant" to his feelings, interests, and wishes as he insisted time and again.[14]

Washington and his fellow delegates to the convention sensed that they were living in unusual times. John Adams was right in perceiving that they had "been sent into life at a time when the greatest lawgivers of antiquity would have wished to live." Few people in history, Adams wrote, had enjoyed the opportunity to create a new government for themselves and their posterity. There was a special bonus, too: fame. Participation in this world-historical experiment held out the promise of eternal glory. What surer way to build a lasting monument to oneself than to contribute to the founding and consolidation of the republic?[15]

And yet it would take courage as well as conviction to entrust one's eternal reputation to a political experiment that, if history was any guide, might easily fail. If the American experiment failed, what then? Washington would have sacrificed the reputation that was most precious to him.

It was time for constitution making.

On May 13, 1787, bells chimed and exuberant crowds cheered as the Philadelphia Light Horse escorted George Washington into town. Robert Morris, the superintendent of finance during the Revolutionary War, invited the general to stay in his fine brick mansion, staffed with servants in livery and a French butler. For twelve fretful days Washington waited until a quorum was present, spending his leisure time dining with the Morrises, Benjamin Franklin, and other Philadelphia notables "in great Splendor."[16]

When the meeting finally began in the high-windowed first-floor chamber of the State House on May 25, a rainy and gloomy Friday, Washington's imposing appearance—in his striking general's uniform—moved all the delegates present. Here was the American Revolution in flesh and blood. They unanimously elected him to the presidency of the convention. With his usual modesty, Washington thanked his colleagues, reminding them of the "novelty" of their collective enterprise and asking for their indulgence "towards the involuntary errors which his inexperience might occasion."[17]

The convention was indeed a novel enterprise: it was the most audacious—and revolutionary—example of political planning in the Western world. No small dreams, no cautious methods for the delegates in Philadelphia. They wanted nothing less, Washington wrote, than "radical cures."[18]

During the sultry Philadelphia summer, flies buzzing in the motionless air of the State House, a body of fifty-five men—"an assembly of demigods," Jefferson commented from Paris—deliberated and self-consciously set about designing a national government in a grand manner and for all time. Together they brought vast experience, Enlightenment educations, common sense, optimism, and a willingness to experiment, to create, as Alexander Hamilton would say, "good government from reflection and choice." They succeeded magnificently. For four months, six days a week, from ten o'clock in the morning until four in the afternoon, they would labor, pausing only once for a ten-day recess during which a committee on detail consolidated the convention's work.[19]

The inviolable rule of the convention was secrecy. No news whatsoever was to filter out. Even the windows of the first-floor chamber in which the members met, it was reported, were nailed shut. Nothing could justify such concealment, Jefferson huffed, "but the innocence of their intentions, and ignorance of the value of public discussions." On the contrary, secrecy made it possible for the Framers to debate and deliberate freely, oblivious to public opinion, free of pressures from onlookers, constituents, or newspapers. For his part, Washington was determined to enforce the policy. One day, finding a delegate's notes on convention proceedings haphazardly left behind, he delivered a stern lecture. "I must entreat gentlemen to be more careful," he scolded. "I do not know whose paper it is, but there it is, let him who owns it take it." Washington bowed and left the room with a dignity so severe, commented William Pierce of Georgia, that every person seemed distressed. "For my part," Pierce recalled, "I was extremely [alarmed], for putting my hand in my pocket I missed my copy of the same paper, but advancing up to the table my fears soon dissipated. I found it to be in the handwriting of another person."[20]

The Framers had a clear understanding of the power that the new national government would need. Following the broad outlines of James Madison's "Virginia Plan," they agreed on expanded authority for the national government, to which the states would now be subordinate. They had no doubt that the new federal legislature would be the engine of law and policy. Still, they were unwilling to permit it to "absorb all power into its vortex," as Madison said. They decided that there would be two legislative chambers, the lower one based on popular representation, the upper one based on equality between large and small states. Slaves would be accorded three-fifths representation. Slavery was implicitly sustained: union, order, and national strength were far more important to most of the Framers than were the rights and liberties of black men and women. Still, they tried to elide the brutal reality of slavery, never introducing into the Constitution the words "slave" or "slavery," referring instead to "persons held to service or labor" and "all other persons." They designed a federal judiciary that would hold at least enough power over the political branches to protect its own independence. And there would be a separation of powers, a system of checks and balances among the branches of government, blunting the power of any "oppressive" majority and ensuring stability if not inertia in government. But what about Washington's formula for energy in the executive branch of government?[21]

The shape of the new national executive confounded the delegates. Colonial leaders had already had a bellyful of executive interference and bullying from royal governors and other minions of the Crown. Thus, during the Revolutionary War, most states had either executive councils (the twelve-member executive council in Pennsylvania was typical) or weak governors with no veto power. New York State was virtually alone in having a strong chief executive—in the person of the seven-term governor, George Clinton. Endlessly the delegates puzzled over the authority of the executive. Just a few months earlier Madison had admitted to Washington that although he knew that a national executive would have to be provided for, he had scarcely given any serious thought to how it should be constituted or with what powers "it ought to be cloathed."[22]

The Framers debated at length the basic issue—a single or collective executive. The "New Jersey Plan" proposed a weak, plural executive chosen by Congress. Edmund Randolph, the governor of Virginia, strongly opposed a single individual in the executive magistracy, regarding that as the "foetus of monarchy." Roger Sherman of Connecticut as well as Benjamin Franklin agreed, wanting nothing resembling an elective king. For his part, George Mason of Virginia suggested that an executive composed of three men—one from the North, one from the middle states, and one from the South—would "quiet the minds of the people." In addition, he objected to an executive without an advisory council, for that, he contended, would be "an experiment on which the most despotic Governments had never ventured. The Grand Signor himself had his Divan," he said, referring to Turkey.[23]

But others at the convention, like Charles Pinckney of South Carolina, Rufus King of Massachusetts, and James Wilson of Pennsylvania, yearned for a vigorous executive. "In order to control the Legislative authority, you must divide it," said Wilson. "In order to control the Executive, you must unite it." Wilson wanted to see a single executive directly elected by the people and not tied to any council—except a cabinet composed of men of his own choosing. Gouverneur Morris, a member of the Pennsylvania delegation, too, spoke up for a strong executive who, he said, echoing traditional paternalistic monarchical ideas, would be the "guardian of the people"—and, he added significantly, "even of the lower classes." Some wanted the president to serve for a lengthy term in office, thereby hoisting him above the vicissitudes of popularity; others proposed a single seven-year term with no possibility of a second.[24]

On June 18, New York delegate Alexander Hamilton rose to give his ideas about the best form of government. He described an executive who would be elected indirectly by the people and hold his position for life, with an absolute veto on legislation. He would be able to pardon all offenders, traitors excepted. He would have the power to make war or peace, with the advice of the upper house, the Senate. He would make treaties with the Senate's advice, but he would have the sole direction of all military operations; and he would send ambassadors and appoint all military officers. But Hamilton admitted some uncertainty. He was not convinced that a truly effective executive could ever be established on republican principles.[25]

The men of Philadelphia showed an even less firm grasp on the question of how to *elect* the executive. Knowing today the crucial differences between the parliamentary and presidential forms of government, we read the convention debates with suspense as the delegates teeter back and forth among the different options: selection of the executive by Congress, by the state legislatures, by state governors, or by the voters. But the delegates themselves were more impressed by the dilemma than by the drama. Edmund Randolph proposed that the national executive be chosen by the national legislature. Elbridge Gerry of Massachusetts objected, remarking that Congress and the presidential candidates would constantly "intrigue" and "bargain and play into one another's hands." James Madison, too, rejected any collaboration between the legislature and the executive. Gouverneur Morris suggested that if the executive was "to be the Guardian of the people let him be appointed by the people." But others countered that most people were gullible and could be led astray by a "few active & designing men." Some proposed that electors, chosen by the people, select the executive.[26]

No subject at the convention, admitted James Wilson, perplexed the delegates more than the mode of choosing the president. Three times in July delegates approved motions that the executive be chosen by the national legislature—the equivalent of a parliamentary system—but in late August they were back to square one. Delegates rejected every proposal for electing the executive. A Committee on Detail finally settled on the system of electors, and, by that time, the other fatigued and impatient delegates were in no mood to revisit the question again.

How many future presidents of the United States would have loved nothing more than to have been present at the Constitutional Convention, voting themselves all the power they craved. "Oh, if I could only be President and Congress too for just ten minutes!" Theodore Roosevelt would bellow in the Oval Office in frustration, overheard by the visiting Franklin D. Roosevelt. But because Washington presided over the convention, he could not—at least not in the convention itself—play an active part in shaping the executive office that he would soon occupy. In private, Washington did complain, in a letter to Hamilton, that the delegates who opposed strong and energetic government were "narrow minded politicians," and he confessed that he regretted "having had any agency in the business." Still, it was but a passing moment of discouragement. During the formal sessions, he broke his silence on two issues, neither concerning the executive branch. He was reported to have sarcastically proposed, in response to Gerry's motion that no standing army exceed three thousand men, that "no foreign enemy should invade the United States at any time, with more than three thousand troops."[27]

He also addressed the question of whether one congressional legislator should represent forty thousand persons, as the draft constitution had stipulated, or thirty thousand, as a delegate from Massachusetts suggested. Taking a stand in favor of democratic representation, Washington spoke briefly in favor of the proposed change, recommending more "security for the rights & interests of the people"—and his authority and prestige were such that the motion of the representative from Massachusetts was immediately and unanimously accepted.[28]

Though he did not take a position at the convention on the nature of the executive branch, he cast votes along with the other members of the Virginia delegation, and some of his votes are revealing. He voted in favor of James Wilson's motion for a single executive. On the question of the executive's veto power, the convention favored a strong negative that could be overridden only by a three-fourths congressional majority—a colossal obstacle for Congress to overcome, empowering a minority of representatives to block the will of the immense legislative majority and signifying only a slight diminution of the absolute executive veto Hamilton had proposed. When a motion was made to reduce that majority from three-fourths to two-thirds, Washington voted to keep the three-fourths rule, but the motion was passed.[29]

Still, the Hamiltonian conception of the executive—a single, strong, independent chief executive—ultimately carried the day. Such an executive could administer the national government with the energy and vigor that Hamilton had prescribed. Not even an executive council or a cabinet holding independent constitutional authority would saddle the president. Although he would have only a limited veto over congressional measures, the executive veto still represented an important prerogative. The president would exercise initiative and assume responsibility in the making of foreign policy; he would be given authority to conduct war as commander in chief, though not the unilateral power to declare war; he would have no general right to exercise emergency powers, but it was assumed he would act for the national self-defense. He would possess considerable control over his own executive branch through his authorization to make appointments. But the presidency would not be a lifetime position, as Hamilton had desired. Instead, the new president would serve only a four-year term, while being indefinitely eligible for reelection; he would be chosen by electors (elected either by the state legislatures or directly by the voters, depending on state preference) and not by Congress. The odd scheme of the Electoral College, said Madison, seemed to give "pretty general satisfaction" to the delegates.[30]

Perhaps the greatest concession the convention made to Hamilton in the final document was to leave executive power and organization rather undefined, as compared to the long list of fairly specific powers of Congress. Clearly, the executive office would take its shape largely from the men who first occupied it. "It squints toward monarchy," Patrick Henry had cried out in Philadelphia against the proposed presidency, "your President may easily become King." But the Framers did not heed him, partly because they fenced the office in with countervailing powers, partly because they had vast confidence in the man who would obviously be the first president. The powers of the president were great, "greater than I was disposed to make them," admitted delegate Pierce Butler of South Carolina. "Nor, Entre Nous," he continued, "do I believe they would have been so great had not many of the members cast their eyes towards General Washington as President; and shaped their Ideas of the Powers to be given to a President, by their opinions of his Virtue." Of course, Hamilton, too, had assumed that Washington would be the first president. "I take it for granted, Sir," he would soon write, "you have concluded to comply with what will no doubt be the general call of your country." A Constitution had been introduced, he explained, but it would be up to Washington to *establish* it. Hamilton was confident that Washington would give the new government "more consistency than the proposed constitution seems to promise." And indeed, the Virginian would turn out to be almost exactly the kind of president most of the Framers had envisaged.[31]

When the meeting was finally over and the Constitution signed, the delegates repaired, one final time, to the City Tavern in Philadelphia, where they "dined together," Washington noted in his diary, "and took a cordial leave of each other." Then, back in his room in the Morris mansion, Washington quietly, soberly, "meditate[d] on the momentous work which had been executed."[32]

"Be assured [Washington's] influence carried this government," James Monroe jubilantly wrote to Thomas Jefferson in July 1788 after nine states—the required number—ratified the Constitution. Indeed, his mere presence at the convention, as historian Glenn Phelps noted, was his greatest contribution to its success. Though he had rarely participated in the convention discussions, his prestige was sufficient to endow the Constitution with authority. The Constitution was not perfect, Washington admitted, and yet, on the whole, it was the "best Constitution that can be obtained at this Epocha." But the real triumph, he explained to Lafayette, was that delegates from so many different states had all reached consensus. It was, he claimed, "little short of a *miracle*." That unanimity also astonished James Madison, who, in *The Federalist* Number 37, perceived "a finger of that Almighty hand" at work in Philadelphia.[33]

Curiously, the Constitution that was produced by startling consensus incorporated and even enshrined principles of disharmony and conflict, for the new national government had been carefully structured so that branches of government, citizens, and interest groups would collide rather than concur. It was, in other words, an agreement to disagree. But how would the first president—who always stressed the crucial importance of American unity—deal with conflict and dissent in his own executive branch and with growing opposition in Congress?

In 1786, Washington had said that it was a "farce" to believe that Americans constituted a united nation. Now the Preamble to the Constitution announced that "We the People" were conferring legitimacy on a new unified nation. Would the dignified and reserved general be able to give life to the abstract idea of national unity? Would he be able to inspire Americans with feelings of belonging, a love of country, and a shared sense of national purpose? During the convention, he had spoken out for "security for the rights & interests of the people." As president, would he, the wealthy planter and slave owner, speak up for those rights and interests?[34]

Unity, conflict, dissent, equality, nationhood, leadership: how would it all come together?

4

The Grand Experiment Begins

On April 30, 1789, Washington left his residence on Cherry Street in a grand coach drawn by four horses, preceded by troops and accompanied by carriages filled with officials. The procession, greeted by excited crowds lining the streets of New York City, moved west and then swung north toward Wall Street and along Broad Street, finally stopping at Federal Hall, an imposing build-ing with massive Doric columns.[1]

John Adams, the new vice president, led the president-elect to a small, partly enclosed portico, overlooking Broad and Wall Streets. A great cheer broke out from below. "I never saw a human being that looked so great and noble as he does," commented a young woman in the crowd. But Massachusetts politician Fisher Ames noticed that time had "made havoc" upon the general's face.

Robert Livingston, chancellor of the state of New York, admin-istered the oath of office; Washington, looking grave, repeated the words and then lifted the Bible to his lips. "Long live George Washington, President of the United States," Livingston shouted. Above the roar of the crowd and the chorus of church bells came the thunder of salutes from the Battery and the harbor. Washing-ton bowed, turned back into the Senate chamber, seated himself next to the vice president, and then rose to deliver his Inaugural

Address. His voice trembled a bit, his words at times came slowly and indistinctly, but he sounded a note of profound eloquence. Ames confessed that he "sat entranced." "The preservation of the sacred fire of liberty, and the destiny of the Republican model of Government," the president told his listeners, were deeply and finally "staked on the *experiment* entrusted to the hands of the American people."

Washington was now president of the United States. But there was no presidency—just a brief, skeletal outline in the Constitution of executive responsibilities. There was only a man, and it would be up to him to breathe life into an empty shell, to give definition and meaning to the office. And simultaneously it would be largely up to him to breathe life into the idea of an American nation by giving citizens common beliefs, expectations, symbols, and heroes.

Preoccupied with drafting the outline of a government of rational laws and institutions, the Framers of the Constitution had given no thought to the ceremonial function of the executive branch of government. Perhaps if they had adopted the parliamentary model they had favored during most of the Constitutional Convention—that is, a president elected by Congress, similar to a prime minister—they might have felt the need for a titular head of state in addition to the political head of government. Or, as historian Glenn Phelps remarked, perhaps Congress, as the most representative of the three branches, might itself have laid claim to the role of national symbol.[2]

Washington intuitively grasped the multiple dimensions of his executive role, understanding that he would have to fulfill a symbolic as well as a political function, and that, in addition to immersing himself in the nation's day-to-day practical politics, he would also have to stand above politics. It would fall to him to incarnate the values of American society, provide unifying emblematic leadership, and play day-to-day national politics. It would be a breathtaking high-wire act.

The young nation, Washington repeatedly explained, had a *"character"* to establish. The Constitution and its "wall of words" would not be strong enough, he was convinced, to defend the nation against the "sweeping torrent of boundless ambition" or the "sapping current of corrupted morals." Only the sturdy shield of unshakable *character* could truly protect Americans. What was that precious American character if not Washington's own? "I glory in the character of Washington because I know him to be an exemplification of the American character," wrote John Adams in 1785.[3]

What constituted the character that the president would project onto his waiting, receptive country?

In addition to Washington's well-known virtue, integrity, and courage, perhaps the most important element of his character was something stunningly modern: respect for human reason. He always believed that human rationality—tempered by practical experience—underlay the entire American political experiment. "Wisdom . . . aided by experience," he wrote in 1792, would bring the new government "as near to perfection as any human institution ever approximated." Washington possessed faith that his countrymen were "rational beings" who could shape their own social and political destiny. He saw Americans as virtually alone among peoples in their openness to new political ideas and willingness to graft those ideas onto their own experience in politics. "The foundation of our Empire was not laid in the gloomy age of Ignorance and Superstition," he had written to the state governors in 1783, "but at an Epocha when the rights of mankind were better understood and more clearly defined than at any former period." Progress had been made in the "science of government"; new horizons, he wrote, had been opened by Enlightenment research in "social *happiness*," and the fruits of philosophers' labor and wisdom could be "happily applied" to the creation of the new American nation.[4]

Reason and happiness: the two leitmotifs in Washington's writings. Though constitutional government had been established primarily to guarantee order and security, Washington was convinced that his fellow citizens, armed with reason, could attain the far higher value of human happiness. Indeed, Americans, he wrote, had just presented the "Novel and astonishing Spectacle" of a people deliberating "calmly on what form of government will be most conducive to their happiness."[5]

And even more than the happiness of Americans was at stake, for Washington believed that their experiment would "stamp political happiness or misery on ages yet unborn." An isolated, fledgling nation of only four million people, marginal to the great powers of Europe, would serve as a beacon to all peoples. And even this grand project of happiness for all humanity, he believed, was founded in reason. There was a "*rational* ground," he remarked to a friend, "for believing that not only the happiness of my own countrymen, but that of mankind in general" would be advanced by good government in the United States. Happiness for all! Well, not quite all. "It behooves me to prevent the emancipation of [my slaves]," wrote Washington in 1791.[6]

The happiness that Washington envisioned was a dazzling departure from centuries of thought, for it was located in the social and political sphere, not in the afterlife. Happiness required no supernatural intervention. In the century of the Enlightenment, happiness was not a question of redemption, grace, or salvation; nor did it pose problems of guilt, sin, spiritual anguish, human frailty, or the tragedy of the human condition. If Washington personally experienced any disquiet, it stemmed only from a concern for his ability to do his duty, meet his formidable obligations, and protect his sterling reputation.

Happiness was of this world, and yet it did not signify the pursuit of pleasure or conspicuous consumption: Washington underscored that "happiness & splendour" had little in common. For him, happiness was two-pronged; on the one hand, it meant the collective satisfaction of citizens living in a well-ordered civil and political society, under the aegis of a well-administered government "where equal Laws and equal Rights prevail"; and on the other hand, it meant individual citizens enjoying improvements in their lives. For Washington, happiness was more than just a goal: it was the essential *obligation* of government. It was the glue and the promise of the social contract—a truly revolutionary project as well as a major political commitment.[7]

In his first Inaugural Address, Washington summed it all up, pointing to an "indissoluble union between virtue and happiness, between duty and advantage, between the genuine maxims of an honest and magnanimous policy, and the solid rewards of public prosperity and felicity." Here was Washington's formula for happiness: virtuous and reasonable citizens and politicians, accepting and fulfilling their responsibilities to their nation and to others, understanding that the interests of their fellow citizens were inseparable from their own, able to balance their own "advantage" with the common good, would work together for the "solid" reward of prosperity and felicity. Virtue was not its own reward: the reward was happiness.

Nor was the quest for happiness an arduous enterprise. "I think I see a *path*, as clear and direct as a ray of light," Washington wrote to Lafayette in 1789. "*Nothing but* harmony, honesty, industry and frugality are necessary to make us a great and happy people." The young nation was a land of freedom, agriculture, and commerce, and no other country, he remarked, could be more favorable for the happiness of people of moderate capital or, he added, even for "the happiness of the lowest class of people."[8]

The belief in reason that buttressed Washington's deep commitment to happiness did not, however, turn him into a doctrinaire man. Rather, his respect for rationality made him aware of the limitations of reason: he was moderate in expressing his own opinions and open to the ideas of others. Thus for Washington the corollary of reason was not intellectual intransigence but rather tolerance. Should he "set up [his] judgment as the standard of perfection?" he asked rhetorically in his draft notes for his first inaugural speech, perhaps recalling the maxims he had copied out as a boy. "And shall I arrogantly pronounce that whosoever differs from me, must discern the subject through a distorting medium, or be influenced by some nefarious design?" He knew better. "Infallibility not being the attribute of Man," he would later write, "we ought to be cautious in censuring the opinions and conduct of one another."[9]

Washington's tolerance for the opinions of others extended naturally to his commitment to liberty of conscience in matters of religion. He cared not if men were "Mahometans, Jews, or Christians of any sect, or Atheists." Indeed, he went beyond "tolerance," for he explained that tolerance implied merely "the indulgence of one class of people" in permitting others to exercise what were in fact their inherent rights to freedom of religion and conscience. And what of Washington's own religious beliefs? In his writings, he never mentioned Jesus Christ but rather alluded to the "Great Author," the "invisible hand," and "an intelligent and accountable Being," expressions typical of Enlightenment deism. His religious detachment and, as historian Paul Boller remarked, his deist indifference to sectarian quarrels contributed to his respect for freedom of conscience. The paramount value of religion, he would write in his Farewell Address, was its "indispensable" contribution to morality and hence to "political prosperity."[10]

Who better than this rational, tolerant man, who identified with the happiness of Americans, to embody the American "character" on the national and world stage? Theatrical metaphors abounded in Washington's writings; he continually referred to the "theatre of action," the "public theatre" and the "stage." He saw Americans as "actors on a most conspicuous theatre" where would be displayed "human greatness and felicity." And yet he alone would occupy center stage; he alone was the consummate leader and political actor. No one else possessed such mastery and self-mastery. Washington himself remarked that his aloofness was the result of a "studied reserve." "He could, at the dictate of reason, control his will and command himself to act," Gouverneur Morris would similarly recall.[11]

As the public emblem of American character, how would Washington stage his appearances? Understanding that the frail and vulnerable new government needed to be respectable and dignified, and realizing, too, that all of his actions would have "durable consequences," he asked Adams, Hamilton, Madison, and Jay for their "candid and undisguised Opinions." What style of residence was proper for the chief magistrate to live in? How sociable should he be? Should he invite members of Congress to dine with him? Was one day a week sufficient for receiving unofficial visitors? Should he hold several large "entertainments" each year? Would it be appropriate for him to call on others? For his part, Hamilton looked to European courts for wisdom in protocol, recommending that Washington establish the "dignity of the office" and a "pretty high tone in the demeanour of the Executive." Still, aware that "notions of equality" were deeply rooted in American society, Hamilton counseled against "too immense an inequality," suggesting that "frankness and simplicity" might sometimes be the safest route.[12]

Social events in the presidential residence were meticulously choreographed. At his Tuesday afternoon levees, visitors—any men in proper attire who wished to meet the president—were introduced by Washington's secretary, Tobias Lear, to the president. Dressed in black velvet, wearing yellow gloves and a long, polished sword, Washington stood in front of the fireplace and bowed to the guests as they arrived. The visitors then formed a circle around the room. Beginning on his right, the president toured the circle, speaking a few words to each man. He then resumed his position in front of the fireplace; each guest in turn approached him, made his final bow, and left.

These were excruciatingly stiff and formal occasions, some people complained. Washington, too, disliked them and admitted to impatience with "the frivolities of ceremony." Still, he conceived such events as a way to separate his symbolic role from his political role and protect his time for public business. "I could not get relieved from the ceremony of one visit before I had to attend to another," Washington had complained. "In a word, I had no leisure to read or to answer the dispatches that were pouring in upon me from all quarters." His plan to devote a fraction of his week to purely ceremonial duties was self-protective and rational, not pretentious.[13]

Even so, other royal-like flourishes were not lacking: Washington's lordly offer—refused by Congress—to be compensated only for his expenses; in New York, a splendid new house on Broadway—where the president lived and worked—staffed by seven slaves and fourteen white servants; then, when the capital moved to Philadelphia in late 1790, the loan of Robert Morris's mansion, which Washington called "the best *single House* in the City"; the large and elaborate dinners he and Martha gave, with powdered servants standing by; the prodigious amount of champagne and claret the president ordered; the carriage emblazoned with his crest, drawn by six cream-colored horses, in which he augustly traveled alone in formal processions, followed by carriages transporting the chief justice of the Supreme Court and cabinet members; his white horse adorned with fancy saddle and leopard-skin housings; and the grand designs he approved by the French architect and engineer Pierre-Charles L'Enfant for a majestic new capital city on the Potomac, a city of imposing edifices and avenues that, like St. Petersburg, the eighteenth-century capital of Russia, would be constructed by unfree labor.

Was Washington then a closet republican king—or czar? Unlikely. When Colonel Lewis Nicola, during the War of Independence, suggested to Washington that he assume monarchical powers, the general had exploded in anger, replying that no occurrence in the course of the entire war had given him "more painful sensations." He viewed the idea of royal power with "abhorrence" and confessed that he was "at a loss to conceive what part of my conduct could have given encouragement" to such a mischievous plan. But royalism apparently did not disappear with the Constitution. Upon his return to the United States from Paris in 1789, Jefferson was stunned to hear people at dinner parties openly expressing a preference for "kingly, over republican, government." At such social events, Jefferson claimed to have found himself the only committed republican. All that kept these fans of royalism in check, he wrote, was their respect for Washington. It was the president's moderation and virtue, Jefferson believed, that prevented the American Revolution from ultimately subverting the very liberty that it was intended to establish. Historian James Flexner agreed: Washington's "most revolutionary act," he wrote, was his outright refusal even to consider the possibility of joining the ranks of monarchs.[14]

Washington's deep commitment to republican institutions—despite his elegant tastes—did not diminish the enthusiasm of some people for monarchy or silence the criticism of others who derided him as a proto-king. The New York *Daily Advertiser* denounced his "royal pomp and parade." His birthday celebration was a "monarchical farce," proclaimed one paper, while another criticized his "supercilious distance." "He holds levees like a King," sneered the New York *Argus*, "shuts himself up like a King, shuts up other people like a King, takes advice of his counselors or follows his own opinion like a King." It was understandable that men who had just liberated themselves from the chains of European monarchy feared finding themselves shackled again, indeed more understandable than the nostalgia of other Americans for royal rule. Years later, in 1814, an elderly Jefferson would state categorically that Washington was "no monarchist," yet he wondered if the president, with his inclination to "gloomy apprehensions," might have adopted levees and other pompous ceremonies in order to prepare Americans for a possible change to monarchy, should the American experiment fail.[15]

Accusations that he harbored monarchical ambitions surprised Washington all the more since he saw himself and his wife leading restrained if not utterly boring lives. All day he toiled in his modest ground-floor office in his New York residence—and later in his third-floor office in his home in Philadelphia. He even decided that his coach should be "plain and elegant" rather than "rich and elegant." He and his wife shunned "the follies of luxury and ostentation," he wrote to a friend, adding that even their "simplicity of dress" was designed to "support propriety of character." For her part, Martha confessed that she preferred staying at home to the protocol of public appearances. Washington, too, complained about a sense of isolation. So strongly had he emphasized the inappropriateness of his accepting invitations to dinner in private homes, he wrote, that he had not received a single one![16]

Some of his friends defended the president against charges of royal ostentation. One noted that Washington could be seen occasionally walking alone in the streets of New York, while the vice president, Adams, "is *never* seen but in his carriage and six." Though John Adams had in 1785 complained that deference to Washington had transformed the Virginian into the object of a cult that dispensed with people's rational faculties, now Adams changed his tune. "Sir, you have given yourselves a king, under the title of president," the prince of Orange had said to Adams in 1788. "It is true," Adams commented, "and I rejoice in it."[17]

Now Adams insisted that Washington be called "His Most Benign Highness," because, he reasoned, a man could be "president" of any little organization. Washington was annoyed at the attempts "to bedizen him with a superb but spurious title," Madison later recalled. Not Washington but rather others with "vitiated political taste," Madison wrote, favored such "unrepublican formalities." But the voice of republican reason won the debate on presidential titles in the House of Representatives: Washington would be called the "president." "The more simple, the more republican we are in our manners," stated Madison during that debate, "the more rational dignity we acquire."[18]

Washington would not have disagreed with Madison, for the adulation of the crowds weighed upon him. "He looked oppressed by the attention that was paid him," commented one observer in the joyful crowd that greeted the president in Salem, Massachusetts, in 1789. "As he cast his eye around, I thought it seemed to sink at the notice he attracted." When the songs and cheering stopped, he commented, "he bowed very low, and as if he could bear no more turned hastily around and went into the house."[19]

While the admiring crowds reacted to him as if he were a charismatic leader, Washington himself would have coldly dismissed the notion of charismatic leadership. The authority and prestige of a charismatic leader reside not in institutions and laws, but in his magnetic personality as it operates upon the emotions of his followers; his virtually magical power is, by definition, not transferable. But Washington believed in rotation in office, in stable, well-managed government responsible to an enlightened citizenry. And the symbols, gestures, and rituals that he adopted to buttress his staging of American character as well as his staging of the office of the presidency would also be founded in reason.

Unlike the autocratic Napoleon whom artists portrayed dripping in furs, velvet, and jewels, so many emblems of power, the symbols in the most famous portraits of Washington were strikingly restrained. In Edward Savage's 1796 canvas of the Washington family at home, the figures of George, Martha, and two grandchildren, relaxed but serious, are arranged around a table on which lies a map of the new federal city. Gilbert Stuart's portrait of the same year has Washington standing erect, his right arm outstretched in greeting. Though wearing a sword, he is dressed plainly in black. At his right is a writing table on which are pen and ink, books about his military past, the Constitution, *The Federalist*, and the *Journal of Congress*. A glowing rainbow surrounds not the man but rather the republican chair of government. "As a political philosopher," commented historian Garry Wills about this image of Washington, "he engages in a dialogue, not a lone act of creation. Others will sit in his chair and do what he has done. The same authority will be wielded, the same limits observed." Even so, it was not easy for the artist to humanize the president. "Now, sir, you must let me forget that you are General Washington and that I am Stuart, the painter," Stuart said as he tried to put the president at ease. Mr. Stuart, Washington coolly responded, need not forget "who he is, or who General Washington is."[20]

Also staged were Washington's tours of the New England states in the fall of 1789 and of the South in the spring of 1791. As the nation's political leader he wanted to meet with influential citizens while seeing with his own eyes the conditions in the country and gauging the mood of the people. And as the ceremonial leader of the nation, he would make himself visible to citizens as the emblem of national unity and identity. His paramount goal was a national government that would not be remote or abstract but would take on life through him. By presenting himself to the people in controlled, celebratory public events, he hoped that citizens would—through him—transcend their local loyalties and develop an attachment to the concept of their federal government and to the *idea* of a unified American people. "The subordination of a group under a single person," wrote sociologist Georg Simmel, "results, above all, in a very decisive unification of the group." Still, it was not mass emotion that Washington sought to excite. His voyage around the states would be his own rational brand of public theater.

In the fall of 1789, accompanied by two secretaries and six servants, Washington visited all the New England states except Vermont and Rhode Island, which were not yet members of the union. He dutifully dined with the notables, watched parades, listened to songs and odes, received accolades, and strolled in the countryside. But what interested him most was seeing firsthand how the country was functioning and how work was performed.

In Boston he toured a sail manufactory, noticing the twenty-eight water-powered looms at work and the fourteen girls spinning. "They are the daughters of decayed families," he wrote, "and are girls of Character—none others are admitted." At another factory in Boston, he saw that each spinner had a "small girl" to turn the wheel. Though he remarked that the girls worked from eight o'clock in the morning until six o'clock in the evening, he did not comment on the broader social issues of women's and children's labor. In Beverly, Massachusetts, he stopped at a cotton manufactory and admired the new carding and spinning machines, especially one, operated by a single person, that could spin eighty-four threads at a time. In Marblehead, he viewed a fleet of a hundred shipping vessels but wrote that the houses were old, the streets dirty, "and the common people not very clean." Portsmouth had stagnated after the war, but, Washington happily reported, "it is beginning now to revive again." In Springfield, he examined arms and ammunitions depots. In Hartford, he visited Colonel Wadsworth's woolen manufactory and ordered a suit of broadcloth to be sent to him in New York. "There is a great equality in the People of this State," he jotted down in his diary while visiting Connecticut. "Few or no opulent Men and no poor—great similitude in their buildings."[21]

Factories, bridges and roads, crops and fish, gristmills and sawmills, harbors and ships—everything that moved, grew, and made the country work captured his attention—except working people in their singularity. Unlike Jefferson, whose idea of a tour of France was to "ferret the people out of their hovels . . . look into their kettles, eat their bread, loll on their beds under pretence of resting yourself," Washington's diary of his journey is impersonal:

he describes no characters, relates no anecdotes, recalls no memorable individuals, displays little interest in the lives and bread of ordinary Americans.

Touring the southern states a year and a half later, he saw that the South was not as industrialized and prosperous as the North, yet the crops had been good for the past few years, and people seemed in good humor and generally satisfied with their lives and their government. He also felt more at home there, commenting on prosperous people's homes, paying a visit to the widow of his friend General Nathanael Greene. In Charleston, he found people wealthy, gay, hospitable, and happy. As his journey approached its end, he wrote to a friend that the South

> appears to be in a very improving state, and industry and frugality are becoming much more fashionable than they have hitherto been there. Tranquillity reigns among the people, with that disposition towards the general government which is likely to preserve it. They begin to feel the good effects of equal laws and equal protection. The farmer finds a ready market for his produce, and the merchant calculates with more certainty on his payments. Manufacturers have as yet made but little progress in that part of the country, and it will probably be a long time before they are brought to that state to which they have already arrived in the middle and eastern parts of the Union.[22]

While Washington studied the country, the country studied—and applauded—him. That applause served a purpose. Tributes to the first president, commented the British minister to the United States, "tend to elevate the spirit of the people, and contribute to the formation of a *national character*." Americans were the gainers, he concluded, from the recital of the feats of the Revolutionary War and their praise of Washington. As for the president himself, he was pleased with "the marks of respect shewn to my official

Character." He had accomplished his goal. He had fashioned himself into the ideal unifying emblem of the nation. No one else could have played the role as well. While future presidents would be respected because of the office they held, in Washington's case, the office would become respected because of the man.[23]

But would the president be as successful in his political role—in setting up the well-managed government that, he had so often said, would be the guarantee of American felicity?

5

The Transformation

"Who is Mr. Rosecrantz?" an irritated Washington snapped at one of his officials. Without proper authority, this man had presumed to take on business of a public nature. As administrator in chief, Washington insisted on accountability, diligence, and speed. And attention to details, details, details. If the details were mastered, everything else—the big plans and ambitious projects—would follow. Only "systematic and solid arrangements," he wrote, could protect the nation from the hazards of chance.[1]

Irritated that some critical mail had gone astray, he emphasized to his cabinet the necessity of always sending duplicates and sometimes triplicates of important letters. When Thomas Pinckney, the American minister in London, made the singular error of sending a message to Philadelphia in a code to which there was no key, Washington exploded, demanding that Mr. Pinckney's "extraordinary inattention" be quickly corrected.[2]

Convinced that good governance was the result of forethought and method, the president instructed his cabinet officers "to deliberate maturely, but to execute promptly and vigorously. And not to put things off until the Morrow which can be done, and require to be done today." In all situations, including emergencies, Washington demanded calm examination and "a deliberate plan." No action, he repeated to the secretary of war, should be undertaken without absolutely reliable facts and information.[3]

In his first Inaugural Address, Washington had apologized for being "unpracticed in the duties of civil administration," but no one in the United States was more accomplished in executive management than he. His work as commander in chief during the war, remarked historian Douglas Freeman, had been "one-tenth field commander and nine-tenths administrator." Coordinating business with governors, working with political leaders, consulting foreign diplomats, procuring supplies, seeing to an infinite number of operational details, "he had in a certain sense been acting as President of the United States since 1775," observed historians Stanley Elkins and Eric McKitrick.[4]

In orchestrating the affairs of the executive branch, President Washington was a *transactional* leader—managing, supervising, delegating, compromising, mastering the centrifugal forces in the government. But he was more than that, too, for he was leading in the creation of an entirely new political structure. Indeed, to provide strength, coherence, purpose, and personality to the executive branch, he became a *transformational* leader—for he was giving strong institutional shape to an enhanced philosophy of executive leadership as well as inspiring and cementing citizens' commitment to the federal government.

Unlike future presidents who would necessarily have to react to previous presidencies, choosing either to follow the policies and practices of their predecessors or to set a different course, Washington's position was unique. He was faced with few policies to contravene, no traditions to repudiate. In 1789, it was a rare task indeed to set up, almost from scratch, an entirely new government. Aided by the inventiveness, resourcefulness, and pragmatism of men such as Hamilton, Jefferson, and Madison, he alone would set the precedents that future presidents would continue or disrupt. Whether his successors would be less forceful, less active, more majoritarian, or more populist, it was Washington who established the standard for presidential leadership. It is his construction of the office and his rock-solid commitment to the fundamental value of the national government itself that, more than any specific decisions he made or routine acts of management performed, marks his presidency as one of the most formative in American history.

"We are in a wilderness without a single footstep to guide us," fretted Madison in July 1789. But Washington fully grasped the task at hand and felt steely determination more than anxiety. Since absolutely everything he did would establish a precedent, "it is devoutly wished on my part," he wrote to Madison, "that these precedents may be fixed on *true principles*."[5]

One of those principles, Washington noted, was that the Constitution "must mark the line of my official conduct." He was resolved not to exceed the limits of his own executive powers. His aim was "neither to stretch, nor relax from them in any instance whatever, unless imperious circumstances should render the measure indispensable." The reason? He firmly believed that a "spirit of encroachment" would tend to consolidate all the branches of government into one, thus creating a "real despotism." Still, the *definition* of executive powers remained vague but expansive.[6]

Washington's effort to follow the Constitution to the letter sometimes bogged him down. Did the Constitution give the president the power to change the meeting place for Congress in cases of emergency during a congressional recess, he asked his attorney general in the fall of 1793, when a calamitous outbreak of yellow fever shadowed over Philadelphia. Wary of assuming too much power and thus giving "food for scribblers," Washington asked all his confidants for counsel. "What would you advise in this predicament?" he asked Jefferson, Hamilton, Madison, and others. For weeks he agonized about his constitutional authority in this relatively insignificant matter.[7]

Ever respectful of the separation of powers, he often deferred to the authority of Congress. He used his veto power rarely, not when he disagreed with congressional policy—unless that policy concerned military or foreign matters—but rather only when he believed that a constitutional issue was at stake. In this regard, he took on a responsibility that, decades later, the Supreme Court would appropriate for itself. For his part, Jefferson was relieved when Washington finally vetoed a bill in 1792, setting a precedent for future presidents.

Although Madison had designed a system of checks and balances that would place branches of government in adversarial relationships with one another, Washington sought to ensure harmony across the government. Even after senators rebuffed his attempt to consult with them in person, during the summer of 1789, about a treaty he was negotiating with the Creek Indians, he continued to keep the Congress informed about future treaty negotiations. When the Senate asked for background information concerning other treaties with Indians, Washington unreservedly provided all relevant material. When the Senate rejected one of his minor nominations, he suggested to senators that in the future they might communicate their doubts to him so that he could respond, but he did not question their right to reject his nominees. Another symbolic gesture of deference revealed a president who had no intention to act as a peremptory ruler. When he received a packet from the French National Assembly addressed to "The President and Members of the American Congress," instead of opening it, he simply handed it over to the Senate, asking senators whether they would like to open it. After deliberating, the senators decided that Washington should open it and report back to them. Washington's action may have helped him acquire, in the words of historian Glenn Phelps, "a reservoir of political trust that he could draw from in the future when matters more essential to establishing a strong presidency were at issue."[8]

Still, the president did not always defer to Congress. In 1796, when the House of Representatives, objecting to the Jay Treaty with England, asked to review Jay's diplomatic instructions, he would not compromise. He contended that only the Senate had the right to information relating to treaties. The House backed down.

Indeed, the most important principle on which Washington sought to buttress a stable political machine was executive *authority*. While deferring diplomatically to Congress on relatively small, symbolic matters and while not wishing to contravene the Constitution, Washington knew that central to efficient government was a forceful executive. "Energy in the executive is a leading character in the definition of good government," Hamilton had written in *The Federalist* Number 70. "It is essential to the protection of the community against foreign attacks: It is not less essential to the steady administration of the laws, to the protection of property . . . to the security of liberty."

But how to establish a powerful executive branch? The Constitution was far more specific about the powers of Congress than about the powers of the president. It stipulated that the president would be commander in chief of the army and navy, that he could make treaties if two-thirds of the Senate concurred, that he could appoint judges and other federal officers and consult with his own executive department officers. But on other matters the responsibilities and prerogatives of the president were left vague. The Constitution, for example, granted the president no specific power to conduct foreign affairs, though it did grant him the right to receive ambassadors—and hence to recognize nations. This authority was crucial, given the turbulent European situation and the emergence of a revolutionary government in France, which Washington, unlike other European leaders, would recognize. The Framers of the Constitution had been wary of giving the president too much power in foreign relations. Even Hamilton, the advocate of a strong presidency, had noted in *The Federalist* Number 75 that a nation's "intercourse with the rest of the world" should not be left "to the sole disposal" of a president. And yet, by making the president the master of the two key agencies of foreign policy, the diplomatic corps and the armed forces, the Framers had indeed made it possible for the president to seize control over foreign policy. The seeds of the future "imperial presidency" were sown.

The president's power expanded in the summer of 1789, when Congress created the Departments of State, War, and Treasury, placing them not under its own jurisdiction, as they had been under the Articles of Confederation, but instead in the executive branch.

Significantly, one of the most crucial debates regarding the new executive departments concerned not the president's authority to appoint department heads, but rather his power to remove them. The Constitution gave the Senate the power to approve the president's nominations, but did that mean that it also had the right to approve or reject the president's decision to sack a department head? In *The Federalist* Number 77, Hamilton, despite his insistence on a strong executive, had oddly favored giving the Senate the authority to "displace as well as to appoint" executive officers. But others insisted that the removal power had to be left solely in executive hands. "Vest this power in the Senate jointly with the President," Madison warned, "and you abolish at once that great principle of unity and responsibility in the executive department." Suppose the Senate rejected a president's attempt to remove a department head, argued a representative from New Jersey; "what a situation is the President then in, surrounded by officers . . . in whom he can have no confidence?"[9]

The right of removal was a critical issue that undergirded the president's ability to conduct executive business without congressional interference. The president's right of removal passed in the House, but in the Senate it ended in a tie, broken by the vice president. It was a transformational moment. Instead of a presidency compromised by Congress, a tendency toward centralized control in the executive branch began to emerge, one that would pull the cabinet, the vice president, and other parts of the executive branch tightly into the orbit of presidential direction and influence. Despite some of the Framers' fears of one-man rule and despite the numerous obstacles they placed in the path of strong presidential leadership, Washington would shape a powerful executive branch of government that would formulate most of the nation's foreign and domestic policies.

To head the Treasury Department, Washington had the excellent sense to choose Alexander Hamilton, his aide during the Revolutionary War. In 1781, the brash New Yorker had admitted that he felt no friendship for the general, but since then the two men had come to trust each other. In another superb appointment, he invited Thomas Jefferson, still the nation's ambassador in France, to accept the position of secretary of state, and he asked Henry Knox to be secretary of war. The attorney general would be Edmund Randolph, the former Virginia governor. The duties of Hamilton, Jefferson, and Knox were daunting, for they would be responsible for a multiplicity of government offices and services.

Hamilton's department was the most complex. Appointed and confirmed on the same day, he got to work immediately. Not only was he charged with managing the nation's finances—credit, banking, accounting, and the collection of taxes—he also had under his jurisdiction the customs department, the nascent coast guard, lighthouses, and the Post Office. The last, first headed by Samuel Osgood, was of critical importance in Washington's mind, for most news and information, especially about the government, depended on the mail system. "I need not say how satisfactory it would be," Washington wrote, "to gratify the useful curiosity of our citizens by the conveyance of News Papers." As if all those responsibilities were not enough for him, Hamilton asked Congress for the authority to make all purchases for the entire government, though that job would prove so onerous that Congress would soon create a new office, purveyor of public supplies, under the direction of the secretary of the treasury. Congress also asked the treasury secretary to provide regular statements of receipts and expenditures of all public money as well as plans for improving federal revenues.[10]

Hamilton would play a pivotal role in almost all of the decisions made by Washington's administration. "Most of the important measures of every government are connected with the treasury," Hamilton self-assuredly remarked, while Jefferson darkly warned Washington that the Department of the Treasury appeared poised "to swallow up the whole executive powers." Even after Hamilton left Washington's cabinet early in 1795, replaced by Oliver Wolcott, he continued to influence government policy. "Will you favor me with your opinion?" Wolcott would typically write to his predecessor, eager to follow his lead.[11]

It was only after some hesitation that Jefferson accepted the position of secretary of state. "I know of no person, who, in my judgment, could better execute the Duties of it than yourself," Washington wrote warmly to his fellow Virginian. "My chief comfort," Jefferson replied, "will be to work under your eye, my only shelter the authority of your name."[12]

Like Hamilton, Jefferson would enjoy considerable power in the new cabinet. Foreign ambassadors would have to conduct their business with him. When the French minister, the Count de Moustier, wanted to deal directly with the president, Washington explained diplomatically that the "great Departments" had been instituted because he alone could not perform all the business of the state.

In his department, Jefferson proved to be a master manager, asking his ministers abroad for reports twice a month and upbraiding them for inattention. "I will complain not only of your not writing," he admonished William Short in the Netherlands, "but of your writing so illegibly, that I am half a day deciphering one page, and then guess at much of it." Some of the communications problems seem laughable today. Especially egregious was the silence of the minister in Madrid. "Your letter of May 1789 is still the last we have received," Jefferson wrote to him in 1791. Since there was no Department of Justice, the creation of the federal court system—a Supreme Court of six members, with John Jay as chief justice, and thirteen district courts—was also placed in Jefferson's domain, along with supervision of marshals, who were the "handy men" of the federal administration, officers responsible for taking the census, collecting fines, enforcing jail terms, overseeing court procedures. Patents and copyrights also fell under the Department of State, as did an official library, a repository for documents and newspapers, and even the national mint—the head of which, scientist David Rittenhouse, accomplished almost nothing in three years while the country suffered from a shortage of coins.[13]

After the brilliant appointments of Hamilton and Jefferson, Washington's appointment of Knox, who had served as secretary of war since 1785 under the Articles of Confederation, was less satisfactory. Charged with supervising an army of five thousand men, the navy, shipbuilding, the national arsenal, and Indian affairs, Knox was the least talented of Washington's inner circle. Dismayed by Knox's failure to consult and plan effectively, the president peppered him with a barrage of questions and directives that he would have imposed on no other secretary—"By what means . . . ? By what authority . . . ? What certainty is there . . . ? What effect would it have . . . ?"—virtually taking over as armchair commander himself. When Knox was asked his opinion on a matter, Jefferson sneered, he simply mouthed Hamilton's line, admitting "at the same time, like a fool as he is, that he knew nothing about it." The next secretary of war, James McHenry, who had been Washington's aide during the War of Independence, fared no better. McHenry had an affinity for minutiae. Finding him buried under a mountain of details, Hamilton lectured him, but the advice was in vain. "McHenry is wholly insufficient for his place," Hamilton railed, "with the additional misfortune, of not having the least suspicion of the fact!" "Your opinion," Washington replied, "accords with mine." The administrative and strategic ineptitude of Knox and McHenry gave a weak footing to the Department of War, but Washington doubtless had so much confidence in his own military experience that he was willing to tolerate old cronies in this position.[14]

As for the attorney general, though Randolph attended meetings with the cabinet, he had no department of his own: he accepted a retaining fee to give the president legal advice while carrying on his private practice, grumbling that he was a kind of "mongrel." And yet, when he gave his opinion about a policy measure, as Jefferson discovered, he was always half in favor of it and half against it. Randolph, Jefferson wrote, was "the poorest chameleon I ever saw having no colour of his own, & reflecting that nearest him."[15]

An unofficial presidential adviser and key liaison to Congress was Virginia representative James Madison, for Washington trusted no one's judgment more than that of his fellow Virginian. It was Madison who ghostwrote Washington's Inaugural Address, purposefully including the recommendation that Congress consider amendments to the Constitution—the "bill of rights" that Madison and Jefferson were energetically promoting. And it was Madison who composed the official reply to the president from the House of Representatives and then ghostwrote the president's reply not only to the House of Representatives but also to the Senate! In the words of the editors of the Madison papers, Madison "was in dialogue with himself."[16]

The president turned to Madison for advice ("What do you think I had best do?") on a variety of subjects, from proclaiming a day of Thanksgiving to judicial nominations to sending ministers abroad. Once apologizing for being "troublesome" and abusing Madison's time and generosity, Washington warmly wrote, "Ascribe it to friendship and confidence." Not standing on ceremony with his friend, one Saturday he casually invited him and Jefferson "to take a family dinner with me today" to discuss plans for the new federal city. Only after Madison and Jefferson left

Washington's inner circle, in 1793, would Hamilton receive such words of affection from the president.[17]

Left somewhat out of the loop was Vice President John Adams. Perhaps the vice presidency might have evolved into a kind of prime ministership, argued historian Flexner, if Washington had been so disposed and had had more confidence in Adams. But during the Second Continental Congress, the Bostonian had opposed Washington's wish to establish a professional, permanent army, and the two had not been close after that. The vice presidency, Adams sniffed, was "the most insignificant office that ever the invention of man contrived or his imagination conceived."[18]

Alone at the top of the pyramid stood George Washington. Despite his famous diffidence about his abilities, he passionately believed that public happiness would issue from his "obeying the dictates of my conscience." "No fear of encountering difficulties and no dread of losing popularity," he self-confidently announced in 1789, "shall ever deter me from pursuing what I conceive to be the true interests of my Country."[19]

Washington was a hands-on president, and yet his stunning success in establishing a firm and vigorous executive branch of government was not his achievement alone but rather the achievement of the collective leadership of a small, radiant galaxy of men of outstanding intelligence, creativity, and integrity— Washington, Hamilton, Jefferson, and Madison.

All day long, documents and papers traveled back and forth among the president and the department secretaries. "By this means," Jefferson commented, Washington "was always in accurate possession of all facts and proceedings in every part of the Union." At his breakfast meetings with department heads, the papers he had sent them the day before were discussed, Washington listening to and weighing all arguments. Whereas his successor, John Adams, would conduct important negotiations with France without consulting his cabinet, Washington trusted his department secretaries to help him make policy, especially in the early years of his administration, when Hamilton and Jefferson were still on board. During his absences he authorized the three secretaries to hold "consultations" on any problems that might arise, assuring them that they could, without his approval, act on their unanimous opinions. On constitutional questions as well as on policy issues, he consulted with them and sought their advice. The president's inner circle also helped him draft his annual messages to Congress as well as other important papers and addresses. Dissatisfied with his own draft of a certain paper, Washington wrote to Hamilton, "Be so good therefore as to new model, and let me have it (if convenient to you) this afternoon."[20]

Part of Washington's greatness, Gouverneur Morris would comment in 1799, lay in his understanding how to lead *with* others, "how best to use the rays" emitted by the dazzling geniuses of men like Hamilton and Jefferson. Such collective leadership would have reassured the Framers in Philadelphia who feared that a one-man executive would degenerate into monarchy. But did those Framers approve Washington's sending the sitting chief justice of the Supreme Court, John Jay, to London to negotiate an important treaty with Great Britain? Washington saw the presidency, historian Phelps remarked, "as *a part of* an integrated national government, not as an institution standing *apart from* the other branches."[21]

There was only one domain in which Washington assumed sole responsibility: patronage. "I *alone* am responsible for a proper nomination," he wrote. It was an unpleasant, onerous responsibility, as office seekers persisted in knocking on his door. Even Jefferson had to advise people not to importune the president. "To overdo a thing with him is to undo it," Jefferson counseled. But Washington had set up strict guidelines for himself, underscoring his intention to act only with regard to the "public good," dismissing considerations of "blood or friendship." Indeed, when his nephew Bushrod Washington asked his uncle for the position of United States attorney for Virginia, Washington tactfully declined, explaining that the young man had neither the experience nor the standing "of some of the oldest and most esteemed General Court lawyers in your own State, who are desirous of this appointment." Unlike the British prime minister Robert Walpole, who, when charged with corruption in the mid-eighteenth century, wailed, "Have I acted wrong in giving the place of auditor to my son, and in providing for my own family?" Washington was determined to be "exceedingly circumspect." Alluding to the mythological Greek giant with a hundred eyes, he wrote that the "eyes of Argus are upon me."[22]

To fill his government Washington sought men of knowledge, skill, and integrity who also had the respect of their communities, for that, he believed, was the best way to win over the affections and goodwill of the people for the federal government. Still, it was not easy to get qualified men. John Marshall was only one of many who declined positions in the government. "In short," Washington wrote to Hamilton as he searched for a new secretary of state in 1795, "what with the non-acceptance of some; the known dereliction of those who are most fit; the exceptional drawbacks from others; and a wish . . . to make a geographical distribution of the great officers of the Administration, I find the selection of proper characters an arduous duty." Hamilton could offer no cheer. "A first rate character is not attainable. A second rate must be taken with good dispositions & barely decent qualifications."[23]

Washington weeded out the undesirables. The temperamental antics of Major L'Enfant "astonished me beyond measure!" he wrote to Jefferson about the architect of the new federal city, concluding that he had no choice but to dismiss the Frenchman in 1792.[24]

Little by little he anchored the government in the class of educated, established, influential men who prized public service and were well regarded by their communities. Over half of the members of the Constitutional Convention would serve as administrators, legislators, or judges. The result was government by the elite.

Was it also government for the elite? Washington believed that he could encourage citizens' commitment to their national government by standing above politics, above faction, above geographical section. And yet he did not stand apart from the nation's wealthiest citizens. On the contrary, in his appointments as well as in many of his policies, he embraced their interests. Was Washington's administration, Jefferson, Madison, and others began to wonder, betraying the very principles that Americans had fought for in 1776—liberty, equality, and the pursuit of happiness? Indeed, it did not take long for ideological differences among the members of Washington's cabinet team to deepen and for Washington's ideology of unity to unravel.

6

The Deepening Chasm

"It may be interesting for the President to consider whether there ought not to be some *executive impulse*," Hamilton wrote to Washington, suggesting that the chief executive actively embrace the full orbit of national life—from war and peace to the economy—leading, not following. Hamilton had once copied a quotation from Demosthenes: wise politicians, like generals, the Greek sage wrote, should not wait on events to know what measures to take, but rather precipitate events and march at their head.[1]

But Washington was torn between his desire to be an energetic executive and his respect for the constitutional limitations of his powers. "Motives of delicacy," he insisted, restrained him from proposing specific legislation. Even on issues about which he cared most deeply—a national university, canals, agriculture—he made only general statements of vision to Congress. After that, he explained to a friend, "it rests with them to decide what measures ought to be adopted for promoting the success of the great objects, which I have recommended to their attention." On the question of the new Bill of Rights, though he acknowledged that it was "practicable" for Congress to "secure to the people all their justly-esteemed privileges," he did not intervene actively, leaving leadership to Madison in the House of Representatives.[2]

And yet a fundamental reversal would take place in the balance of legislative power between the president and Congress: the executive branch would indeed come to dominate the legislative process. Leadership of Congress would be supplied from outside the House and Senate rather than just from within.

When Hamilton's allies in Congress formally asked him for advice about the nation's economic problems, the activist secretary of the treasury had just the opening he craved: he meticulously compiled impressive reports and proposals on public credit, a national bank, and manufacturing, and intervened in the framing of bills at the start and at the finish and all the way in between. Hamilton's strikingly modern and farsighted policies would shape the economic and industrial landscape of the nation—giving it a mighty push toward becoming a military-industrial giant rather than the self-contained, backwater agricultural and mercantile nation that it might conceivably otherwise have become.

Would Washington's genteel and somewhat vague vision of a politically neutral nation that was inhabited by a happy, prosperous, and enlightened people and offered asylum to the oppressed, promoted manufacturing, supported a national university, and boasted a solid infrastructure of roads, canals, and bridges be overshadowed by Hamilton's ambitious program? Though the president sided with Jefferson as often as with Hamilton when there were divisions in the cabinet, Washington would nevertheless come to acquiesce in the New Yorker's pounding refrain of trade, power, strength. Although the Constitution gave full control for fiscal and commercial matters to Congress, Hamilton reversed the intention of the Framers, seizing the initiative in economic policy. And while Washington's strategy for governing was in harmony with Congress, his administration would nevertheless quickly move a long way from the words of Article I of the Constitution: "All legislative Powers herein granted shall be vested in a Congress of the United States . . ."

. . .

Hamilton's Report on Public Credit, presented to Congress in January 1790, was a typically bold initiative—a plan to establish the sound credit of the country as well as provide a source of capital for significant industrial projects. Hamilton was eager for the new federal government to assume the nation's revolutionary foreign debt, domestic debt, and also the states' debts, totaling well over $70 million. His ideas were forward-looking and creative. "There are epochs in human affairs," he had written in 1780, "when *novelty* even is useful."

"A national debt," Hamilton had remarked to Robert Morris in 1781, "is a national blessing." And yet everything about Hamilton's economic plans sparked contentious debate—even his idea of funding the debt by selling new debt securities. As soon as the first step of the plan was announced—compensating present holders of certificates of debt—objections arose. James Madison wanted only the original owners of the securities, those who had never sold them to speculators, to receive full value. Those people who sold them for a fraction of their worth as well as the speculators who bought them would receive, according to Madison's version of the plan, a lesser value. "Speculation" on the debt, Madison judged, was "wrong, radically & morally & politically wrong." But Hamilton successfully argued that such "discrimination" would render American debt nonfungible in the future. For his part, Washington felt sympathy for the poor veterans and soldiers who had felt obliged to part with their certificates and sell them to "unfeeling, avaricious speculators." And yet he agreed with Hamilton's practical measures. "The subject was delicate," Washington wrote, wishing that Madison, though acting on the "purest motives," had never stirred doubts about Hamilton's policy or even raised the issue of discrimination.[3]

Another source of conflict was Hamilton's plan for the federal government to assume the wartime debts of the states. Assumption was only fair, Washington argued, because the expenses that states had incurred had been for a "common cause." But Hamilton had something other than fairness in mind. With the federal government assuming their debts, the state governments would be left without a reason to levy taxes and would, Hamilton hoped, eventually wither, posing little challenge to a strong central government. But objections arose over assumption, too. When Virginia, having already managed to liquidate much of its debt, opposed the plan, Hamilton sternly warned that "this is the first symptom of a spirit which must either be killed or will kill the Constitution." The debate dragged on for five months in 1790. One day, outside the presidential mansion in New York, a haggard and dejected Hamilton buttonholed Jefferson, urging action on the issue of assumption. Otherwise New England, which still had considerable war debts, might secede. Could Jefferson use his influence with southerners? he asked. Though opposed to Hamilton's fundamental concept of a permanent debt, Jefferson agreed to host a dinner for Madison and Hamilton at which a compromise was hammered out. In exchange for moving the national capital to Philadelphia for ten years and then to a permanent site on the Potomac, Madison and Jefferson promised to help push funding and assumption through Congress. They were apparently as transactional in their opposition to Hamilton's policies as Hamilton was in his grab for influence.[4]

The most controversial of Hamilton's ideas was his proposal for a national bank, presented to Congress in December 1790. The Bank of the United States would be chartered by Congress and its records supervised by the treasury secretary, although the government would hold just a fifth of its capital and appoint only a fifth of its directors. The Bank would not handle ordinary transactions but only major transfers of money. It would service the national debt, assist in collecting taxes, make loans to major private enterprises and to the government itself, and the Bank's certificates of indebtedness would circulate as a kind of supplementary currency in the nation.

At the heart of the plan was a marriage of government and private bankers. The two would be so intertwined in a system of mutual support that each would be financially and legally implicated with the other. The Bank's charter, by specifically preventing it from investing in land and thus helping farmers, restricted it to industrial development. The plan had a divisive thrust. It was divisive socially—inasmuch as Hamilton's aim was to fortify the American union by giving wealthy businessmen a vested interest in the nation's political and financial strength—and it was divisive geographically, for the northern commercial and industrializing states would stand to profit far more than the agricultural states of the South.[5]

The debate fired up again in 1791, as opponents of the Bank focused on the issue of constitutionality—appropriately perhaps, now that Congress was meeting in Philadelphia, the site of the Constitutional Convention. Madison again led the charge against his old friend Hamilton, his collaborator on *The Federalist*, his partner in conceiving and setting up the new government. After expounding on the drawbacks of the bank plan—a run on the Bank could be calamitous; several banks would be better than one—Madison declared that the great charter had given the government no authority to incorporate a bank. Indeed, the bank bill, he authoritatively said, "was condemned by the silence of the Constitution." But supporters of the Bank held their ranks and passed the bill in its essentials.[6]

Would Washington sign it? Attorney General Randolph and Secretary of State Jefferson both advised against it. But Hamilton was undaunted, laying out a broad construction of the Constitution, calling the Bank vital to the nation's economic interests, and asserting that, under the Constitution, Congress possessed the right to use all means "necessary and proper" to realize objectives that were not forbidden to it. His argument echoed the words Madison had written only a few years earlier in *The Federalist* Number 44—that "wherever the end is required, the means are authorised; wherever a general power to do a thing is given, every particular power necessary for doing it, is included." With whom would Washington side? The president, Hamilton had once said, "consulted much, resolved slowly, resolved surely." After delaying as long as he could, the president decided in favor of Hamilton and signed the bank bill.[7]

When scrip—that is, certificates entitling the holder to buy shares in the Bank at a later date—went on sale in the summer of 1791, people hungry for quick profits flocked to purchase them, and it was immediately oversold. In a month the value of a piece of scrip rose from $25 to $325. A virtuous republic was being buried in "scrippomany," Jefferson wrote, excoriating "the rage of getting rich in a day." It was a "scramble for so much public plunder," Madison agreed, bemoaning the "daring depravity of the times." But Washington was pleased: the sale of scrip, he noted, proved not only that people had confidence in the government but that many Americans too had surprising economic resources.[8]

Was Washington duped by Hamilton, as some of Hamilton's critics charged? Hardly. The president claimed never to put his name to a bill that he did not truly approve, but he admitted that he did not understand the fine points of finance and banking and did not disguise his lack of interest in both of them. And, unlike Hamilton, who wanted to retire no more than 2 percent of the principal per year, Washington seemed to want to retire as much of the principal as possible. Even so, he embraced Hamilton's agenda because he concurred with it. Indeed, the public credit of the United States stood on such solid ground, he happily crowed in 1791, "which three years ago it would have been considered as a species of madness to have foretold." As far as the president was concerned, Hamilton's economic policies helped chart a path toward his goal of national cohesion and strength.[9]

There was even more to Hamilton's economic agenda. The House of Representatives had asked the secretary of the treasury for a plan for the "encouragement and promotion" of manufacturing that would make the United States independent of other nations for essentials and particularly for military supplies. After almost two years of evaluating the nation's capacities and needs and reflecting on the question, Hamilton revealed in December 1791 his plan for the kinds of economic measures that he believed would guarantee the nation's industrial power for decades to come. His key proposals were for governmental aids to business, subsidies, bounties for inventions, a variety of internal improvements, and the encouragement of immigration of manufacturers and workmen. He envisioned a manufacturing base in the North that would draw on southern raw materials, and he coldly approved making women and children more "useful" by adding them to the labor force in factories. After all, nearly four-sevenths of workers in British cotton factories, he blithely reported, were women and children "of whom the greatest proportion are children and many of them of a very tender age."[10]

Hamilton was no acolyte of laissez-faire economics, which he impatiently dismissed as a "wild speculative paradox." He demanded government intervention, government regulation and planning, government stimulation of business. "There is at the present juncture a certain fermentation of mind," he wrote in his report, "a certain activity of speculation and enterprise which if *properly directed* may be made subservient to useful purposes; but which if left entirely to itself, may be attended with pernicious effects."[11]

But here the president stood his ground. Washington intuitively sought a balance between agriculture and industry. On the one hand, he relished describing to his friend Lafayette the "spirit of enterprise that prevails" in America. He marveled at factories springing up in many states. Commerce, he noted, would improve "human manners and society," uniting mankind "like one great family in fraternal ties." But though he was becoming more and more urbanized, even citified, land was still in his blood, and he clung to his belief that agriculture, represented by the self-sufficient, independent yeoman, was "of primary importance" to the young republic.[12]

Thus, on Hamilton's proposals to promote manufacturing, Washington demurred. They did not "come within the Powers of the General Government," he crisply wrote, nor "comport with the temper of the times." Passing over the specifics of Hamilton's report, he dismissed it on constitutional, procedural grounds. Hamilton's vision and goals were not discussed; and, though it accepted many of his recommendations about tariffs, Congress never voted on Hamilton's plan. It was virtually his only defeat while treasury secretary. But Hamilton's visionary report had made an impression on Washington, who would come back to the theme of federally sponsored industry in his eighth and final Annual Address to Congress, noting that, while manufacturing "on public account" was "inexpedient," the government did in fact have an obligation to ensure production that was "essential to the furnishing and equipping of the public force in time of War."[13]

With the exception of the Report on Manufactures, Washington and Hamilton worked in harmony together. Indeed, the model that Hamilton consistently sought to promote was that of presidential government—a government in which an active, vigorous president, dominating the legislative process, upsetting the carefully contrived balance of powers between president and other branches, was curbed less by formal constitutional restrictions than by the pressures and exigencies of the political arena—by what the people, or their leaders, would bear at the moment. The essence of Hamilton's political tactics, as he plotted to enact his fiscal measures, was primarily the exertion of influence—regardless of constitutional theory and principle. There were no clear limits on his power, though some organized opposition to him was rising in Congress. But for the most part it was only Washington's lack of enthusiasm for some of his proposals that set the parameters.[14]

Above all, Hamilton wanted action. He wanted to precipitate new realities, to create a strong state with a powerful central government that planned the nation's economic future. Unlike so many sleepy and stagnant administrations in the nineteenth century, Washington's government bubbled over with innovation, experimentation, and controversy. Through Hamilton, the executive branch came to dominate much of the legislative agenda. "Nothing is done without him," groused Senator William Maclay of Pennsylvania, noting that it was "totally vain" to oppose one of his bills. Congress might as well go home, for "Mr. Hamilton is all-powerful, and fails in nothing he attempts." The "Executive, or rather the Treasury Department," pronounced Representative John Mercer of Maryland, was really the *efficient Legislature of the country*, so far as relates to the revenue, which is the vital principle of Government."[15]

Like Washington, Hamilton was a transforming leader. Disdaining incremental change, he sought to transform the country's economic landscape purposefully, radically, lastingly. Was it a coincidence that revolutionaries in France awarded Hamilton—and not their old Francophile friend Jefferson—honorary citizenship? But while Washington had begun his presidency with a gentle vision of a prosperous, peaceful, educated nation, Hamilton had grander and more practical things in mind. History had taught him that republics were not pacific; on the contrary, they were no less "addicted" to war than monarchies. "No government could give us tranquillity and happiness at home," he had declared at the Constitutional Convention, "which did not possess sufficient stability and *strength* to make us respectable abroad." In *The Federalist* Number 11, he painted a startling vision of American might, of a republic that would "baffle all the combinations of European jealousy to restrain our growth," a republic superior to all "transatlantic force or influence," one that would dictate a new balance of power.[16]

"We are the embryo of a great empire," Hamilton wrote in 1795. His goal was to solidify American strength and prosperity while the nation matured in a peaceful environment from infancy to manhood. Only then could it blossom and "exercise the greatest portion of strength of which it is capable"—that is, assume the role of a powerful military nation-state. "If we can avoid War for ten or twelve years more," he wrote, "we shall then have acquired a maturity, which . . . will authorize us on our national discussions to take a higher & more *imposing* tone." And his economic strategy would lay the groundwork for American military ascension. "What true Englishman," Hamilton remarked, turning to the people whose government and economy he most admired, "does not rejoice that [Great Britain] is able to employ so powerful an instrument of Warfare." Perhaps the great political sociologist Alexis de Tocqueville can offer insight into Hamilton's two-pronged state-building strategy. "All military geniuses like centralization, which increases their forces," Tocqueville wrote, "and all centralizing geniuses like war, which obliges a nation to concentrate many different powers in the hands of the State."[17]

Did the president disagree with Hamilton? "If we desire to secure peace," Washington said succinctly in 1793, "it must be known, that we are at all times ready for war." Though his vision of the nation seemed less aggressive and more defensive than Hamilton's, he came to share Hamilton's emphasis on American might, differing with the New Yorker only about the number of years it would take for the nation to nurture it. "Twenty years peace," Washington noted in 1796, combined with "our remote situation," would "enable us in a just cause, to bid *defiance* to any power on earth." While waiting for the nation to evolve into a mighty military state, Washington prudently subscribed to the maxim of a British friend, that the best strategy for the young nation was "to be little heard of in the great world of Politics."[18]

But was something missing from Hamilton's vision—some

social component, some moral ideal? His new economy would bring force and prosperity to the nation, but how widely would that prosperity be shared? For whom was the new economy and national strength being developed? Hamilton excelled in a series of hard-nosed and innovative policies as well as in outmaneuvering his opponents, but he did not articulate the long-range goals of those policies beyond the power of the state. Or did he simply believe in the power of the state for its own sake? In the hundreds of pages he wrote, he rarely if ever mentioned equality or freedom—beyond the freedom to engage in economic activity and acquire wealth and property. And politically deaf or insensitive, he neither tried to refute the impression that he was an inegalitarian oligarchist nor sought to assure Americans that his policies were related to the republic's most cherished values and ideals. In short, his overriding strategy pertained not to a vision of the welfare of average citizens or to a republic dedicated to the pursuit of happiness but only to the power of the state itself.

It was Madison who sounded the alarm. On December 5, 1791, the same day that Hamilton presented his Report on Manufactures to Congress, Madison published—anonymously—an article entitled "Consolidation" in the new opposition newspaper, the *National Gazette*. He warned of the growth of the power of the federal government and pointed to the "encreasing splendour and number of prerogatives" of the executive branch that might "strengthen the pretexts for an hereditary designation of the magistrate." While resisting the consolidation of power in a central government, Americans should pursue a different kind of consolidation—that of "mutual confidence and affection of all parts of the Union" along with respect for checks and balances. Thus would citizens be prepared to resist oppression and "*consolidate* their defence of the public liberty."

In other *National Gazette* articles, Madison repudiated the Hamiltonian vision of America as a nation-state of military as well as economic might. Madison idealistically proposed that "universal and perpetual peace" could be assured by subordinating government to the will of the people, to the will of those who are taxed, not those who spend, those who constitute the armed forces, not those who direct them. Madison tackled Hamilton's economic policies, too. In his pointed essay "The Union, Who Are Its Real Friends?," he wrote that the nation's real friends are those who consistently oppose "a spirit of usurpation and monarchy" that seeks to "pervert the limited government of the Union into a government of unlimited discretion." Capitalist exploitation and predatory wealth were not yet expressions in the English language, and so Madison resorted to the strongest epithet available with which to flail Hamilton's policies: *monarchist*. In Madison's mind, monarchy and excessive wealth went hand in hand. The "genius of Monarchy," he had written a year earlier, "favored the concentration of wealth and influence at the metropolis."[19]

More anonymous essays in the *National Gazette* poured from Madison's pen, essays in which he reminded his readers of the importance of political and economic equality and suggested that this could be achieved by withholding "unnecessary opportunities" from the "few" and by thwarting their quest for an "unmerited accumulation of riches." Extreme wealth, he argued, should be reduced "towards a state of mediocrity" and "extreme indigence" raised toward a state of "comfort." He claimed that Hamilton and his allies constituted a party that was "partial to the opulent" and sought to govern through "the pageantry of rank, the influence of money and emoluments, and the terror of military force," while he and his own allies were committed to governing in the interest of all. As though he were a shadow treasury secretary if not a shadow president, Madison offered alternative economic policies, an alternative social agenda, an alternative vision of national purpose—all the makings of a different kind of administration.

"The plot thickens," Hamilton wrote to Vice President John Adams, drawing his attention to Madison's articles. By the spring of 1792, Hamilton recognized that battle lines had been drawn, with Madison metamorphosed into "the head of a faction decidedly hostile to me and *my* administration." But he would also soon charge that it was Jefferson, though a member of the cabinet, who stood behind Madison as the real head of the opposition and who had helped establish the opposition newspaper in which Madison's essays appeared. Parties were indeed crystallizing. Madison's anti-Hamiltonian faction, noted Hamilton's ally Fisher Ames, functioned as "a regular, well-disciplined opposition party."[20]

Though Jefferson made no public statements opposing the administration in which he still served, and though he and Hamilton had worked harmoniously together on a variety of measures in the past, in the late spring of 1792 Jefferson decided to take his gloves off. In a letter to Washington, he, too, condemned Hamilton's economic policies for introducing a spirit of gambling, vice, and idleness that undermined American "industry & morality." The New Yorker's ultimate object, Jefferson charged, was to change American government into a monarchy. He explained to the president that he and his friends who were Hamilton's opponents constituted "the republican party, who wish to preserve the government in its present form." Indeed, Jefferson's and Madison's allies would henceforth be known as "Republicans," while Hamilton's partisans would be called "Federalists."[21]

In vain Washington tried to calm his fellow Virginian. In a meeting with his secretary of state, Washington insisted that although "there might be desires," there were no such "designs to change the form of government into a monarchy." The president stressed that it was the incendiary pieces in the *National Gazette* that could produce the "anarchy" that might end in a "resort to monarchical government."[22]

Of course, what Jefferson considered corruption and gambling were Hamilton's forward-looking, hard-hitting, brilliant statist policies. The widening abyss between their deeply held, antithetical visions of American society presaged the emergence of two contrasting political ideologies that would dominate American politics for at least two centuries. Federalists like Hamilton wanted to keep capital concentrated in the hands of the small class of men who would develop the American economy, create factories, jobs, and a powerful, urbanized nation. Madison and Jefferson and other Republicans believed that the government should aid ordinary citizens, farmers, and small manufacturers in a democratic republic that would remain primarily rural. More contradictions may have abounded in Jefferson's ideas than in Hamilton's—contradictions about agriculture and industry, states' rights versus the role and power of the federal government, and, of course, slavery—and yet he possessed an overriding vision, a simple though powerful faith in the people, in the superior right of a majority over a minority. In the eighteenth century, Jefferson's emphasis on liberty and equality appeared loftier than Hamilton's statism and more inspiring to average voters than Washington's dispassionate message of political unity, and, by the end of the decade, it would prove to be more suited to the political and social aspirations of the American people, more able to give meaning to their everyday lives. "Jefferson, eclipsed in the cabinet by Hamilton—the natural democrat against the natural aristocrat—began the mobilization of the masses against the aristocracy of the few," Franklin Delano Roosevelt would write approvingly in 1925—though F.D.R. would find himself embracing Hamiltonian means to achieve Jeffersonian ends.

For their part, Hamilton and Washington were convinced that the conflict was not about philosophy or class but grew from regional differences and parochial localism. The line between the southern and the eastern interests, Washington noted, was stronger than he would have wished. But Federalist Theodore Sedgwick of Massachusetts may have had more insight into nascent class resentments, remarking that Madison had made himself the leader of the opposition, standing "at the head of the discontented in America."

At least there was no opposition within the cabinet to the president himself. Unlike Madison who, as the fourth president, would be confronted by a vice president breaking tie votes in the Senate against him and whose leadership would be impeded by a weak and mediocre cabinet, Washington retained the respect of the members of his administration. Years later, Jefferson credited Washington with averting deadlock and inaction in the cabinet, even though its "monarchists" and "republicans" could not have been more divided and even though he and Hamilton were "daily pitted in the cabinet like two cocks." Washington's strategy, Jefferson recalled, was to encourage his cabinet members to express their views and then decide the course to be pursued and keep "the government steadily in it, unaffected by the agitation."[23]

And yet, despite Jefferson's rosy view and despite Washington's wish for loyal government employees, deep ideological fault lines cut through Washington's administration. There may have been a consensus on constitutional government itself, but there was consensus on little else. Coming into office without an explicit agenda, without a clear and forceful vision for the nation's future, Washington had not needed to assemble a unified team. On the contrary, he wanted an inclusive administration that could profit from the talents of the nation's greatest men. Still, though the ideological diversity of his cabinet did not immobilize Washington's administration, it did weaken it as well as distract and discompose the president.

Washington would later invite—unsuccessfully—the anti-Federalist Patrick Henry to accept the position of secretary of state in his cabinet, and future presidents would, on occasion, similarly appoint to their cabinets men with their own agendas and power bases (Wilson would appoint pacifist William Jennings Bryan as secretary of state, and F.D.R. would pick Republican

Henry Stimson to be secretary of war). But the great theorist of the presidency, Alexander Hamilton, had always taken a dim view of "diversity of views and opinions" in the executive branch. In *The Federalist* Number 70, he had written that "no favorable circumstances palliate or atone for the disadvantages of dissension in the executive department." Dissension could only counteract the "vigor and expedition" he wanted to see in the executive. Washington agreed. Differences had to be subordinated to the common good, or, he predicted, "everything must rub; the Wheels of government will clog; our enemies will triumph. . . . Melancholy thought!"

In the summer of 1792, the president had finally had enough of managing the deepening conflict within his cabinet. He wrote a stern letter to Jefferson. "Without more charity for the opinions and acts of one another in Governmental matters," he lectured his fellow Virginian, "it will be difficult, if not impracticable, to manage the Reins of Government or to keep the parts of it together." Because he deeply valued both Jefferson and Hamilton, he counseled "liberal allowances and mutual forbearances" and an end to "wounding suspicions and irritable charges."[24]

The following day, he composed another letter, this time to reform his other protégé, Alexander Hamilton. More dispirited than severe, the president repeated his message that "internal obstructions" in the government were "harrowing our vitals." He hoped that Hamilton and Jefferson, men of vast abilities as well as "upright intentions," would strive to compromise, to find a "middle course." How could they be so sure their own opinions were correct? After all, mortals possessed no "*infallible* rule by which we could *fore* judge events." Like a gentle doctor, Washington hoped that "balsam may be poured into all the wounds which have been given." But it was becoming increasingly difficult, he confided to Edmund Randolph on that same day, "to keep the machine together."[25]

Indeed, there was nothing conciliatory in Jefferson's reply.

Days after receiving Washington's letter, he responded with a detailed catalogue of his grievances against Hamilton, at the end of which he expressed his determination to resign shortly from the government and return to private life in Monticello. His farm, his family, and his books all called him irresistibly, he wrote.[26]

Hamilton's response was more generous, offering to help Washington "smooth the path" of his administration. "If any prospect shall open of healing or terminating the differences which exist, I shall most cheerfully embrace it." But sandwiched in between Hamilton's pacifying phrases was his own attack on Jefferson. Presenting himself as the "injured party" and a "silent sufferer," he accused Jefferson of organizing a party in Congress "bent upon my subversion."[27]

Washington was puzzled that men he knew to be completely devoted to the republic could be so ideologically divided, remarking oddly to Jefferson that he was persuaded that, at bottom, there was "no discordance" in Jefferson's and Hamilton's views. The president was equally mystified by the absence of tolerance and civility. He himself had always shown respect for the opinions of others. Only through "good dispositions, and mutual allowances" was effective government possible. But as much as Washington strived to be the harmonizer of the group, no accommodation was ever found.[28]

It was all becoming, indeed, a bit too much for the president. Not only did Washington have to cope, as would future presidents, with a proliferation of agencies, departments, and responsibilities, the physical challenge alone was taking its toll. The disunion in his cabinet was the last straw. Collective leadership was breaking down.

On May 5, 1792, responding to a note sent that morning, James Madison entered the president's office. For months Madison had been anonymously attacking Hamilton's policies in the *National Gazette*. Now Washington asked for his trusted friend's advice: with the second presidential election to take place six months later, would the younger man advise him how and when he should announce to the country his intention to retire from office?

The strain and exhaustion showed on Washington's face, Madison wrote in his notes on the meeting. The president complained that he was becoming deaf; his sight was weakening, too. There were troubling lapses in his memory; illnesses had plagued him in 1790 and again in 1791; and now, he sighed, he found the fatigues of his position "scarcely tolerable." Attacks and abuse from the press both surprised and disheartened him; the divisions within his own cabinet posed a "fresh source of difficulty"; and, more and more, he sensed discontent among the people. Nor was he convinced that he alone was indispensable to the effective administration of the government.

The president admitted to Madison that his disinclination to remain in office was "becoming every day more & more fixed." After a lifetime of public service, he longed to return to his farm, "take his spade in his hand, and work for his bread." An alarmed Madison protested that Washington's retirement would give a "surprize and shock to the public mind." While he understood the "severe sacrifice" the president had made for his country, he insisted that Washington was simply the only person who could conciliate and unite the opposing factions. In the present unsettled condition of the young government, Madison concluded, no possible successor to Washington could perform as well in the presidency. No one else had demonstrated such consistently wise judgment. In short, the consequences of Washington's leaving office "ought not to be hazarded."[29]

Unconvinced and disappointed, the president also consulted with Jefferson and Hamilton. For once they agreed. "The confidence of the whole union is centered in you," Jefferson wrote. "North & South will hang together, if they have you to hang on." Hoping to soothe the weary president, he suggested that perhaps Washington would not have to complete a second term—a year or two more of his leadership might be enough to stabilize the nation. "The greatest evil, that could befall the country at the present juncture," Hamilton concurred, would be Washington's retirement from public life, significantly adding that a premature departure would also be injurious to his reputation. The only path open to Washington, Hamilton wrote, was to heed the voice of his country, and that voice, Hamilton promised, "will be as earnest and as unanimous as ever."[30]

Washington expected no less. Competition for political office held no appeal for him. He was willing to make sacrifices for the country, to serve the people, and even to accept another four-year term—but certainly not to engage in a contest for office. The reluctant candidate never threw his hat into the ring in 1792; on the contrary, only by his public silence did he indicate that he would not refuse the highest office. He took no part in the election process.

In November 1792, Washington was elected to a second term with 132 electoral votes. Every elector in the Electoral College had cast a vote for him. While there was no overt opposition to the president, Republicans were not lulled into acquiescence. Rather, flexing their political muscles, they decided to aim their blows at the vice president instead. To oppose the "monarchical" Adams, they chose Governor George Clinton of New York and produced 50 electoral votes for him to Adams's 77.

For Washington, his unanimous election was not a first: he had been unanimously elected commander in chief of the revolutionary army in 1775, unanimously chosen president of the Constitutional Convention in 1787, and unanimously elected president of the United States in 1789. The first two American presidential elections and inaugurations resembled coronations more than political contests. He "would have experienced chagrin," Washington admitted in 1793, had he not been returned to the presidency by "a pretty respectable vote." Still, as he told Jefferson, he was resigned to continue in the "extreme wretchedness of his existence while in office."[31]

Jefferson would quit the cabinet in January 1793; Hamilton would resign from the government in 1795; and Madison would become the recognized head of the opposition to Washington's administration. The loss of Jefferson and Madison from among Washington's advisers and confidants left the president the poorer, for, abandoning him to elitist Federalists, they took away from him any hope for a message more inclusive, egalitarian, and encompassing than that of the political unity of the nation and the power of the state. "Through what official interstice," Madison asked Jefferson, "can a ray of republican truths now penetrate to the President?"[32]

7

The Wider World

It has been said that during his first term Washington taught his successors how to be president and during his second term how not to be president. This is a half truth at best. Better to record that during his first term in office, he set up the executive branch of government, transformed the economic landscape with modern, forward-looking policies, successfully presided over the quarreling members of his cabinet, united diverse states and populations behind a new unified government and his own administrative and symbolic leadership. But better to grant, too, that while forging ahead with his vision of unity and prosperity, he never was quite capable of including in his concept of the people the "lesser" breeds or elements—the abjectly poor and uncouth and uneducated, hosts of American Indians, and slaves, including his own.

And better to grant that during his second term, though he established the executive branch as the sole formulator of the nation's foreign policy, his own foreign policy, no less than some of his domestic policies, polarized citizens and spurred the development of political parties. Despite his unrivaled grasp of the interplay of ambitions and interests, Washington never fully understood the vital need for parties and partisanship as the only way, in the long run, to organize safely and creatively the grand conflicts inevitable in a healthy, dynamic democracy.

•   •   •

Leaving questions of credit and banking largely to his secretary of the treasury, the president had his own priorities for the nation: unity, security and order, and economic development—goals that, in his mind, were interdependent and inseparable.

Unity for Washington meant binding the states together through their commitment to the federal government as well as through trade. Internal commerce among the states, he believed, would "exterminate prejudices" and increase the "friendship of the inhabitants of one State for those of another." *Order*, the sine qua non of civilized society, referred to Americans' respect for the nation's laws. *Security* entailed the right of Americans to navigate freely on the Mississippi; the evacuation by the British of their northwest posts; the settlement of the West without depredations by Indians; peace and friendship with European nations without entanglements in their wars. *Economic development* called for fair trade with Great Britain, access to her ports in the West Indies, the ability to export American products freely and to trade with France. While the goal of economic development would call for skillful negotiations with Great Britain, France, and Spain, the goal of security would require armed intervention against the Indians; and the goal of order would result in Washington's crushing the "Whiskey" rebels in western Pennsylvania. Time and again, Washington would reveal himself a master of realpolitik, adept at seizing and wielding power—but at a price.[1]

Most important to Washington was the peaceful settlement of the Ohio Valley, the southern frontier, and other outlying regions. At stake were not only unity, security, and economic expansion but also, in Washington's mind, the underlying moral strength of America. For he was convinced that American character and virtue would exist in their purest form in the West. While "luxury, dissipation, and corruption" would eventually infect the great cities on the Atlantic, he believed that the western states would retain their "primoeval simplicity of manners and incorruptible love of liberty." How then to protect the orderly settlement of the West from Indian depredations?[2]

The new government considered the Indians "independent powers" and felt obliged to deal with them through treaties. It also recognized Indian ownership of tribal land and sought to buy as much of it as its agents could persuade the Indians to sell. This was American policy in a nutshell: negotiation, land purchases, shows of liberality, guarantees of protection from encroaching whites, and assurances of trade and education. But the Indians saw it differently: for them the deadly pattern was one of white advance, Indian defense, white retaliation.

For his part, the president insisted on moderation, patience, and justice, expressing sincere concern for the Indians' plight. Because the "poor wretches" and "ignorant Savages" had no newspapers of their own through which to air their grievances, he wrote, only one side of the story—the white side—was known. Thus he wanted to "establish a conviction, in the minds of the Indians, of our love of justice and good faith." Government agents "will not be suffered to defraud you," he assured the chiefs of the Seneca Nation, "or to assist in defrauding you of your lands, or of any other things." Recognizing that settlers were encroaching upon Indian territory, he insisted to the Indians as well as to his attorney general that treaties would be held sacred and infractors would be punished exemplarily.[3]

And yet American policy was not so straightforward. White Americans had a "responsibility of national character," wrote Secretary of War Knox to Washington, to treat the Indians "with kindness, and even liberality." But in his official report to the president on Indian affairs in 1789, Knox recommended land purchases—Congress would soon appropriate $20,000 for the purpose—and noted that as white settlers approached Indian territories, the game on which the Indians' sustenance depended would grow scarcer, making the Indians more inclined to sell their land.[4]

Though the president stressed peaceful negotiations with the

Indians, he was ready, as a last resort, to turn to force. In 1790, after General Arthur St. Clair, the governor of the Northwest Territory, was unable to negotiate an end to clashes between white frontiersmen and Indians, Washington sent an army of about two thousand men, led by Colonel Josiah Harmar, into the Ohio territory. The result was a disaster for the Americans. Washington ordered preparations for a new offensive, this time led by St. Clair himself. St. Clair's expedition was even more catastrophic; almost half his force—six hundred men—were slaughtered, exposing the administration to harsh criticism in Congress for its aggressive policies. In a peace move, the president invited fifty chiefs of the Six Iroquois Nations to negotiate with the Americans in Philadelphia in June 1792. But while promising fairness and negotiations, two months later, Washington persuaded Congress to raise five thousand troops and told Knox to "proceed as if war was inevitable."[5]

By the spring of 1794, the Americans were ready. Washington sent out General Anthony Wayne, and in August his four-thousand-strong army decimated Ottawas, Shawnees, and other Indians at the Battle of Fallen Timbers in the Ohio River valley, finally breaking Indian resistance to white settlement north of the Ohio. The next year, Indians from thirteen tribes ceded over twenty-five thousand square miles of eastern and southern Ohio for $25,000 and a $9,500 annuity. Washington conferred a medal on one of the Indian chiefs; it depicted the American commander in chief in martial attire, presenting a peace pipe to an Indian chief, while, in the background, a white man broke the land with a plow. That image captured Washington's preferred notion of American policy.[6]

Indeed, a paternalistic and perhaps farsighted president ultimately seemed to favor some form of assimilation for his Indian "children." Just as he believed that "the *enlightened* policy of the present age" would bring happiness to "all men," he hoped "an *unenlightened* race of Men" might benefit from "rational experi-

ments" that would bestow on them "the blessings of civilization."
His own rational plan for Indians was that, as the game on their
hunting grounds grew ever more scarce, his "beloved Cherokees"
and other Indian nations would become agricultural people, culti-
vating corn, wheat, and cotton, and raising cattle and sheep—privileged occupations that, he emphasized to the Cherokee Nation,
he himself would soon take up once again at Mount Vernon. The
savage Other, in Washington's scenario, would become a Virginia
planter.[7]

Hardly seven years after Shays's Rebellion in western Massachusetts resulted in a constitutional convention, turmoil in Kentucky
and western Pennsylvania seemed once again to threaten American order and security. This time the violence was provoked by
farmers irate at the federal excise tax on distilled spirits. After an
eruption of gunfire and two deaths at the home of a local excise
collector followed by mob violence, Hamilton, who wanted the
government to "appear like a *Hercules*," counseled an immediate
resort to military might. Washington agreed, reasoning that if "a
minority (a small one, too) is to dictate to the majority there is an
end put, at one stroke, to republican government." The president
steeled himself for a quick, decisive end to this challenge to American government—or rather to *his* government. For there was a
personal element in Washington's reaction. "Neither the Military
nor Civil government shall be trampled upon with impunity," he
wrote, "whilst *I* have the *honor* to be at the head of them."[8]

Did the federal government, though, possess the power to
quash the revolt? Article IV of the Constitution stipulated that
federal troops could be used "against domestic Violence" only at
the request of a state. The Pennsylvania legislature was not in session, and the governor, Thomas Mifflin, believed that the matter
could be handled adequately in the courts. Washington, however,
was convinced that the judiciary was no match for "the treasona-
ble fury" of the mob and decided to skirt Article IV by asking for a

judicial writ, permitting him to call up the militias of four states to enforce federal law.[9]

It was a remarkable scene: the sixty-two-year-old president, in full military attire, the martial embodiment of the federal government's authority to enforce national order, riding on horseback to western Pennsylvania in the fall of 1794—the only president ever to lead an army in the field. With him marched more than twelve thousand troops—as well as the man who was the principal target of rebel fury, Alexander Hamilton, the original excise man himself, whom the president, in an impolitic move, had named "acting secretary of war."

In reality, the Whiskey Rebellion was never a true rebellion: it was oratory, mass meetings, and whiskey itself that largely kept the rebels going. The protesters were scattered, their leadership divided. And if there had been an attempt to evade the excise tax, there had been no attempt to overthrow the government. Despite the spectacular military overreaction, no armed confrontation between the farmers and militia ever took place. Not a "drop of blood" was spilled, Washington boasted. Instead, some rebels were arrested, two were convicted of treason. Convinced that the two miscreants had "abandoned their errors," the president used, for the first time, his constitutional power of pardon. "Moderation and tenderness," he decided, were not inconsistent with the public good. He was following Hamilton's recommendation in *The Federalist* Number 74: "A well-timed offer of pardon to insurgents or rebels may restore the tranquillity of the commonwealth." Hamilton's counsel of amnesty would similarly prove useful for President Lincoln, who pardoned Civil War deserters as well as supporters of the Confederacy, and for President Carter, who pardoned Vietnam War draft evaders.[10]

The insurrection "could never be found," Jefferson scoffed. The whole performance, he wrote, "is too humiliating to excite any feeling but shame." But Washington felt triumphant, pleased that now the Europeans would see that "republicanism is not the phantom of a deluded imagination: on the contrary, that under no form of government, will laws be better supported, liberty and property better secured, or happiness more effectually dispensed to mankind."[11]

When it was all over, Madison expressed relief that the insurrection had been crushed so easily, thereby thwarting any attempt to establish the principle that a standing army was necessary to enforce the laws. But Washington had nevertheless created the precedent that, in response to threats to domestic order and constitutional government, power and force would be concentrated in the hands of the most vigorous and single-minded branch of government.[12]

The triad of unity, security, and prosperity applied to foreign relations, too, and would involve the president in delicate negotiations with England and Spain.

How could Americans continue their westward expansion while Spain, in possession of Louisiana, west Florida, and east Florida, controlled navigation and trade on the Mississippi? Spain seemed bent on expanding its sphere of influence; not only was the Spanish government inciting Creek Indians to depredations against white American settlers, there were also signs of a murky conspiracy to set up an independent state friendly to Spain in the territory between the Mississippi and Yazoo Rivers.

Washington had long felt that the tide of history was on the side of the United States in its westward drive. No power on earth, he wrote in 1786, could ultimately deprive the growing American population of the use of the Mississippi. His policy was "neither to relinquish nor to push our claim to this navigation" and meanwhile to open all other possible waterways—he envisaged a canal linking the Ohio and Potomac Rivers—between the Atlantic states and the West. Still, by the time he became president, he realized that it was not enough to count on the momentum of American expansion. A diplomatic solution for the Mississippi would have to be found, and, in 1792, hoping for an agreement from which, he said, both the United States and Spain would derive "reciprocal advantages," he sent William Short to negotiate in Madrid.[13]

But there was no progress. After two years, negotiations with Spain were in a state of "complete stagnation," Secretary of State Randolph complained. That same year Americans in Kentucky and Pennsylvania finally demanded action to secure their right to navigate and trade on the Mississippi. Stung that the government seemed indifferent to their plight, Pennsylvanians sent a letter of protest to the president, contending that, while citizens on the Atlantic coast prospered, westerners were "kept in poverty." "Attachments to governments," they warned, "cease to be natural, when they cease to be mutual." The specter of Kentucky's separation from the union alarmed the president, and, several months later, after the Pennsylvanians' veiled threat to take matters into their own hands and attack Spanish Louisiana, Washington finally acted. First he sent an envoy to calm the situation and then dispatched Thomas Pinckney as Envoy Extraordinary to Spain, where he successfully concluded the Treaty of San Lorenzo in 1795. Spain granted the United States the "privilege" (not the "right," the Spanish underscored) of sailing freely on the Mississippi and using the port of New Orleans.[14]

Was this important treaty the result of Pinckney's bold and skillful tactics? Of Spain's weakness after a series of defeats at the hands of the French revolutionary army? Or, as one historian argued, of the strong character that Washington had conferred on the national government? Probably all of the above. But as Americans in Kentucky and Pennsylvania saw it, a lukewarm president, resenting the demands of protesters whom he regarded as a Jacobin fifth column, had been slow to lead and respond to their needs. Hamilton and Knox had even advised him to ignore the petition. Its language was "exceedingly reprehensible and improper," wrote Attorney General William Bradford. But recalling that citizens possessed the constitutional right to petition the government, he advised against prosecution and suggested it was better to treat the protest "with the contempt it deserves."[15]

Washington's instinct had been to dismiss boisterous public opinion. Even so, he ultimately succeeded in securing for Americans the right to ship their crops and products on the Mississippi. The West would be bound to the rest of the nation through trade and prosperity: unity had been achieved and a crucial navigable avenue for commerce obtained.

Washington had few illusions about international relations. "It is a maxim founded on the universal experience of mankind," he had written in 1778, "that no nation is to be trusted farther than it is bound by its interest; and no prudent statesman or politician will venture to depart from it." As president, he had hard-nosed priorities for America's relations with other countries: self-interest, self-interest, and self-interest. His doctrine, summed up in his Farewell Address, was not complicated: "Nations as well as individuals, act for their own benefit, and not for the benefit of others, unless both interests happen to be assimilated."[16]

The young republic would be faced with a critical foreign relations dilemma when revolutionary France declared war on Great Britain in February 1793 and when the British responded with a blockade of France, their ancient foe. The Treaty of Amity and Commerce, signed by the Americans and the French in 1778, had stipulated that the two nations would defend each other against England. Would Americans now spring to the aid of France in her war against the British? Or would the president suspend the treaty, as Hamilton urged?

In his first Inaugural Address, Washington had underscored that the foundation of his domestic policy would be the "immutable principles of private morality." He did not say that those principles would apply to international policy. Indeed, in 1796 no less than in 1778, he remained convinced that "there can be no greater error than to expect, or calculate upon real favours from Nation to Nation." But what about the invaluable naval and military support the French had delivered to Washington in Yorktown?

France "has not such a claim upon our gratitude as has been generally supposed," Washington would write in 1797. But in the early 1790s, Washington still felt friendship for France. True, he had diagnosed, not incorrectly, an excess of zeal among the French. In a 1790 letter to his friend the Comte de Rochambeau, he recalled that, during the War of Independence, French troops in Rhode Island "burnt their mouths with the hot soup, while mine waited leisurely for it to cool." The affair of the hot soup, he wrote, illustrated "how immoderately you thirsted for the cup of liberty." Still, Washington remarked to Jefferson in late 1792 that "there was no nation on whom we could rely at all times but France." A month later, he called France the *sheet anchor of this country*," and, knowing how sympathetic Jefferson was to the French Revolution, asked him to return to Paris as the American minister.[17]

And yet Washington's head, not his heart, would determine his policy. On April 23, 1793, he proclaimed American neutrality, "a conduct friendly and impartial towards the Belligerent Powers." Neutrality would apply not only to the government but also to individual citizens who could be punished for "committing, aiding or abetting hostilities" against any of Europe's belligerents. Even the passionately pro-French Jefferson, who had wanted to use the promise of American neutrality as a bargaining chip to extract concessions from Great Britain, reluctantly acceded to the prudent new policy. "I fear that a fair neutrality will prove a disagreeable pill to our friends," he wrote to Madison, "tho' necessary to keep out of the calamities of a war."[18]

Still, Washington's hardheaded foreign policy and his fondness for France were not mutually exclusive. For even while announcing his policy of neutrality, he continued to express affection for France. Indeed, in May 1793, against Hamilton's recommendation, he received the young French minister Edmond Genet, thus recognizing the revolutionary government that had just guillotined its hapless monarch. So unwilling was the president to alienate the revolutionary government in Paris that, even as he tried, through unofficial channels, to secure the release from prison of his dear friend Lafayette, he declined in May 1793 to receive Lafayette's brother-in-law who had arrived in the United States with other counterrevolutionary émigrés.[19]

Did the president have the authority unilaterally to declare neutrality? Or did such a declaration belong to the Senate? Hamilton and Madison, writing as "Pacificus" and "Helvedius," debated the issue in a series of newspaper essays. Madison contended that the Senate's power to declare war logically included other policies relating to war and peace. Hamilton, always eager for an expansive interpretation of presidential power, countered that congressional powers to ratify treaties and declare war were mere exceptions to the president's overall responsibility for foreign policy. Still, he conceded that circumstances might sometimes allow for "concurrent authority" in Congress, which would presumably oblige both branches of government to cooperate and collaborate in policy making. Did that mean that the two branches of government could simultaneously declare war and peace? asked Madison. Hamilton's idea, the Virginian wrote, was "as awkward in practice, as it is unnatural in theory." And yet, as Arthur Schlesinger, Jr., has pointed out, Madison was unable to explain how a constrained executive could conduct foreign affairs.[20]

Washington's neutrality proclamation prevented the young nation from becoming entangled in a European war, though it did not create a precedent for such unilateral presidential declarations. Rather, Washington soon invited Congress to "correct, improve or enforce" his neutrality policy, not only making Congress a partner in his program but unwittingly leaving to it future declarations of neutrality—such as those of the 1930s. Even so, Washington's proclamation marked another stage in the consolidation of executive control over foreign policy. The president had received the news of war in Europe at Mount Vernon on April 8; rather than convene a special session of the Senate, he met with his cabinet in Philadelphia on April 19, and four days later he issued his proclamation. He had seized the initiative and swiftly formulated national policy.[21]

American neutrality signaled not only the administration's priority of national self-interest but also the deepening of Federalist conservatism. While many American citizens ecstatically hailed the French Revolution, calling one another "citizen" and "citizenness" in the new French style; while Madison complained that neutrality was a "most unfortunate error" that wounded "popular feelings by a seeming indifference to the cause of liberty"; and while even Washington continued to criticize "outrageous" British policies and express affection for France and his French friends, refusing to forward to the French minister the dry and abrupt missives written by Hamilton, his administration began to lean toward Great Britain. The reasons were multiple—a combination of factors including Hamilton's pro-British stand; the departure of the Francophile Jefferson, the one cabinet member most able to counter Hamilton's realpolitik; the machinations of the volatile French minister Genet who, before an exasperated Washington demanded his recall in August 1793, had successfully conspired to violate the policy of neutrality while also whipping up public feeling in favor of the French Revolution, encouraging the formation of "Democratic Societies," and inciting hostility to Washington.[22]

Unlike Jefferson, who exuberantly believed that the liberty of the whole earth depended on the outcome of the revolution in France, Hamilton felt only contempt for the French project of exporting revolutionary fervor. In the French Assembly's offer, in November 1792, of fraternal assistance to other peoples wishing to recover their freedom, Hamilton discerned "a general invitation and encouragement to revolution and insurrection," a step that would surely "disturb the repose of mankind." Whereas an idealistic Washington in 1792 had expressed the hope that the enlightened policies of the late eighteenth century would bring freedom and happiness to all, Hamilton had no such universalizing impulse. "Every nation," he wrote, "has a right to carve out its own happiness in its own way." Only a decade after the end of the War of Independence, "revolution" had become a scare word for Hamilton and his Federalist allies. Without compunction they repudiated America's founding friendship with France as well as—according to Jefferson—the essential principles of the American Revolution.[23]

"We have already been too long subject to British prejudices," Washington wrote to Lafayette in 1789. The president would have strenuously denied that his administration's policies favored that empire. On the contrary, his catalogue of grievances against Great Britain was long. The British, he bitterly complained, were "without scruple," refusing to fulfill their obligations under the peace treaty of 1783. They had never evacuated their posts on the northwestern frontier; they refused to provide restitution for slaves taken during the war. They permitted American goods to enter the British West Indies only if they were carried on British ships; and they were seizing American ships that traded in the French West Indies. After Gouverneur Morris's attempt to negotiate with the British had ended in failure in 1791, Washington continued to rail against Great Britain. "Can it be expected," he asked, "that there ever will or can be any cordiality between the two countries? I answer, 'No!' "[24]

And yet, in formulating foreign policy, Washington chose Alexander Hamilton for his guide, a choice that would inevitably tilt American policy toward Great Britain. "We think in English," Hamilton had famously written. But it was more than a common language that predisposed the New Yorker to admire everything

English. "What a wonderful spectacle Great Britain exhibits," he wrote. "Observe the mature state of her agricultural improvements under auspices of large Capitals . . . her navigation and external Commerce . . . the huge & varied pile of her manufactures . . . View her in fine the Creditor of the World . . . her public funds are a principal pillar of this astonishing edifice." It was not surprising that Hamilton wanted to buttress his economic designs with a pro-British foreign policy. He had even suggested giving to British Canada use of some navigable section of the Mississippi. "The remedy," Washington snapped, "would be worse than the disease."[25]

In the spring of 1794, amid fury against England and enthusiasm for the revolution in France, the president sent John Jay, the chief justice of the United States, to negotiate with Great Britain, asking Hamilton to draft Jay's diplomatic instructions. But when, a year later, Jay signed a treaty in London in which the British had made few concessions to American claims, Washington expressed dismay and for three months tried to keep its contents secret.

The treaty stipulated that the British would evacuate their northwest posts, but this was virtually their only outright concession. Britain would permit American ships to trade in the British West Indies only if the vessels were under seventy tons (Madison commented that Americans would have to trade in canoes); England did not accept Washington's policy of neutrality and would continue to capture American vessels carrying "contraband" for France; Britain did not give up the practice of the impressment of American sailors or agree to compensate Americans for the slaves "stolen" and liberated during the Revolutionary War—though Americans were obliged to repay their revolutionary debts to English creditors; England could impose tariffs on American exports while she herself would enjoy "most favored nation" status in the United States.

Jay recognized that his work would not give "universal satisfaction," but was unprepared for the furor. In the Senate, Republicans attacked the treaty as "dishonorable" and a "betrayal." Still, in June 1795, the Senate ratified the treaty, though withholding approval of the article limiting tonnage of American vessels. But when the agreement's contents were made public that same month, the outcry was deafening. In New York a mob burned a copy of the treaty in front of Jay's house. When Hamilton attempted to defend the pact at a public meeting, people booed him, and a few hurled stones. In Philadelphia demonstrators smashed the windows of the British minister's home, burning the treaty on his doorstep. In Boston harbor, a British ship was set ablaze. Jay was hung in effigy. As he himself remarked, he could have made his way across the country by the light of his burning effigies.

Madison blasted the treaty's "insidious hostility" to France, asserting that it forfeited American neutrality. Jefferson called the treaty "nothing more than [an] alliance between England & the Anglomen of this country against the legislatures & people of the United States." Protest meetings were held; handbills extolled France as America's solid friend whereas Britain was denounced as the "universal Foe of Liberty." Resolutions condemning the agreement poured in to Washington's office. "No answer given—the address too rude to merit one," he scribbled on a petition; "Tenor indecent—no answer returned," he wrote on another. Newspaper articles called for his impeachment, and illustrators depicted him on the scaffold of a guillotine. Washington was shaken, perplexed at the torrent of abuse directed against him, at accusations that he headed a British faction. Even his revolutionary triumphs were disparaged. "With what justice," demanded one critic, "do you monopolize the glories of the American revolution?"

Federalists shot back that the opposition was the creature of a violent Jacobin party. Merchants and chambers of commerce defended the treaty, predicting that it would bring public prosperity. During the summer of 1795, at Washington's urgent request, Hamilton wrote more than two dozen newspaper essays, defending

the treaty point by point. He argued that Americans should seek
to close and heal the breach between the United States and Great
Britain, for the alternative was war. Washington was pleased with
the articles, and yet he hesitated to sign the treaty.

That July, Britain began seizing American ships. Unbeknownst
to Washington, England, suffering from grain shortages, was determined to stop American vessels carrying grain to France and
insisted on the right to capture enemy property carried aboard
neutral vessels. From Paris, Ambassador James Monroe commented
that England, threatened with famine, "would have refused us
nothing, & we have yielded every thing." Secretary of State Randolph, too, pushed for reopening negotiations with England and
delaying final ratification until England stopped seizing cargoes of
grain.[26]

Then, the bombshell. Returning from a brief vacation in Mount
Vernon to Philadelphia in July 1795, prepared to consult a final
time with his cabinet before making a decision on the treaty, the
president was greeted by his secretary of war, Timothy Pickering.
"That man in the other room," Pickering blurted out, referring to
Randolph, "is a traitor." The smoking gun was a dispatch written
by the French minister, Jean Antoine Fauchet, intercepted by the
British and handed over to the new secretary of the treasury,
Oliver Wolcott. That evening Washington sat down to read it.
Composed a year before, at the time of the Whiskey Rebellion, it
contained a blistering critique of the policies of his administration. Washington's temper rose as he read Fauchet's denunciation
of Hamilton's "immoral" taxation policies and his accusation that
the American government deliberately provoked the Whiskey
Rebellion in order to justify a large standing army. And then, reading on, he saw references to the "precious confessions of Mr. Randolph," who had apparently confided in his French counterparts
and, the dispatch suggested, also made "overtures" to Fauchet. The
information was vague, but Fauchet hinted that there was a question of "some thousands of dollars" and wrote that "the con-

sciences of the self-proclaimed patriots of America already have their price." Randolph had apparently been egregiously indiscreet, but had he also sought a bribe from the French—perhaps, as Fauchet mysteriously suggested, to subvert the military response to the Whiskey rebels?[27]

The next morning, August 12, 1795, Washington hastily announced to his cabinet that he would sign the treaty, as ratified by the Senate. Then, a week later, he confronted an unsuspecting Randolph. "Mr Randolph! here is a letter which I desire you to read," said the president coldly, "and make such explanations as you choose." Randolph could only stammer a few sentences in his defense and then cried out that he "could not continue in the office one second after such treatment" and fled the presidential mansion. With only the incomplete and vague dispatch and no hard evidence that Randolph had sought a bribe, Washington probably rushed to judgment, discerning treason in Randolph's pro-French sympathies. And yet, a few months later, Randolph would write a hundred-page "vindication" of himself that left even friends like Madison puzzled and disappointed.

On the heels of Randolph's supposed betrayal, the president had abruptly decided to accept Jay's treaty. Opposition to the treaty had boomeranged, and the president concluded that it was more prudent to approve the treaty "than to suffer matters to remain as they are, unsettled."[28]

And yet even after his decision Washington continued to smolder with resentment against Great Britain. Only two weeks later, he railed at England's "domineering spirit" and the "outrageous and insulting conduct of some of her officers." In late December, in a letter to Gouverneur Morris, the president dwelled on his grievances toward the British. It was difficult to maintain a policy of neutrality, he wrote, "at a time when the remembrance of the aid we had received from France in the Revolution, was fresh in every mind" and when Americans could easily contrast the "affections" of the French with the "unfriendly disposition of the British government." Indeed, when the French government presented him with a gift of the tricolor flag in January 1796, Washington effusively thanked the French minister. Revolutionary events in France, he wrote, had produced in America "the deepest solicitude as well as the highest admiration. . . . Wonderful people! Ages to come will read with astonishment the history of your brilliant exploits." "The harangue of the President," Madison gloated, "must grate the pro-British party."[29]

In the spring of 1796, the Republican-dominated House of Representatives jumped into the act, threatening to withhold appropriations to put the treaty into effect and demanding that the president turn over copies of Jay's diplomatic instructions. Indeed, a few months earlier Jefferson had expressed the hope that the "popular branch" of the legislature would find a way to "rid us of this infamous act." But for Washington, the demand for documents "not only brought the Constitution, to the brink of a precipice, but the peace happiness and prosperity of the Country, into eminent danger." When the Framers gave the president and Senate the power to make treaties, he insisted, it was not their intention to give the House a veto on their decision. "A crisis now exists," wrote Federalist representative Fisher Ames, as the House and the president locked horns, "the most serious I ever witnessed." Though some Republicans complained that the president was demonstrating "monarchical privilege," the tide turned when Ames made an immensely effective and emotional speech, and the House went on to pass the necessary appropriations for the treaty. There remained no doubt that the president was the formulator of American foreign policy. He had refused to yield to popular pressure or to opposition in the House. Indeed, the idea that the president needed the sanction of Congress to make foreign policy, Hamilton would later remark, was "preposterous."[30]

Did Washington make the right decision in signing the flawed Jay Treaty? He knew that he held no trumps in his hand: England possessed a monopoly on commercial might. And yet he did not lose the game. American commerce would flourish as a result of the Jay Treaty; after the British finally evacuated their northwest posts in 1796, new settlements—Cleveland, Dayton, Youngstown—quickly sprang up. "Since the treaty," Ames happily remarked, "we see nothing but blue sky."[31]

Even so, in accepting the treaty, Americans sacrificed a "measure of their own national self-esteem," observed historians Elkins and McKitrick, though had they rejected it, they would have "sacrificed their own material prosperity." And so the nation swallowed it, but with an accompanying "crisis of spirit." Along with that, the treaty brought an escalation of tensions with the French that would lead to the so-called "quasi war" with France, while the differences with England left unresolved by the treaty would be among the causes of the War of 1812—problems that would confront Presidents John Adams and James Madison.[32]

While the president perceived himself high above the domestic political fray—a man "who is of no party, and whose sole wish is to pursue, with undeviating steps, a path which would lead this Country to respectability, wealth and happiness"—he could not grasp that, in truth, he did not stand above party, but that his foreign policy ideas, like his general outlook, were in fact Federalist. He had only to look around himself to see that, after Randolph's resignation in 1795, he was surrounded solely by Federalists—and second-rate ones at that: Pickering at State, James McHenry at War, Oliver Wolcott at the Treasury. Indeed, after Randolph left, the president stated categorically that he would not "knowingly" appoint anyone to his administration "whose political tenets are adverse" to his administration's policies, for that, he continued, "would be a sort of political Suicide."[33]

Estranged from Jefferson, Madison, and Randolph, the president fell into the conservative Federalist orbit, surrounded by his own ideological team. One advantage of the situation was that he was able to create in the executive branch a stable ideological environment. The disadvantage was that the agenda of his cabinet, still stressing unity, order, prosperity, and might, still implying deference to an elite ruling class, seemed remote from the interests and aspirations of ordinary Americans and contained few ideas that could inspire and galvanize them.

Federalists and Republicans were not only divided over the year-to-year strategy and the everyday tactics of government, they were profoundly divided over ideology and sentiment, over their sympathies for Britain and France, over the kind of nation they were trying to build, over the kind of people Americans should become, over America's political and symbolic place in the world.

Ordinarily, attitudes over foreign and domestic policy are not necessarily congruent; persons combining with one another over domestic issues often split over foreign policy. But in the 1790s, congruence was intensifying in the Federalist camp as well as among Republicans.

The result was a sharpening and hardening and deepening of attitudes separating and polarizing the Federalist and Republican groupings—a polarization that helped produce enormous popular participation in the debates over foreign policy but that confounded the president. And though Republican leaders almost as much as Federalists feared, spurned, and despised the idea of faction and party, their polarization laid the foundations for a powerful two-party politics. What other way was there for Madison and his like-minded friends to oppose Hamilton's policies and the entrenched Federalists than to organize politically? Hamilton had unwittingly become America's first party builder, for his radical policies galvanized the opposition. And unbeknownst to Washington, Jefferson, and Madison, as well as to Hamilton, a long ideological war in America had just begun, the shape of which could not be fully divined during Washington's presidency.[34]

In February 1796, the House, dominated by Republicans, soundly defeated a motion to adjourn for a half hour so that representatives might congratulate the president on his birthday.

Washington found himself in an unknown and bewildering land—one of personal attacks, shrill opposition, and nascent political parties. The Jay Treaty had ignited a spark that left much that was precious to Washington—national unity, the common good, his own reputation—in tatters. He had tumbled down to the level of mortals.

8

The Curtain Falls

Following a Virginia-style breakfast of tea, coffee, and cold boiled meat, the president chatted with his company. It was July 1796 at Mount Vernon; Washington was spending most of the summer on a much-anticipated working vacation away from Philadelphia. Standing on the steps of the west door of his home, he spoke about a subject dear to his heart: a national university, a university of the United States. He had designated land for it in the federal city under construction and had personally offered a substantial endowment. But, speaking "as if he felt hurt upon the subject," one of the guests recalled, he said that there had been little interest or enthusiasm. A year earlier Washington had also described for Jefferson his vision for a national university: it would offer students the opportunity to attend congressional debates, "thereby becoming more liberally, and better acquainted with the principles of law and government." As for the faculty, he hoped that some of the luminaries of the Scottish Enlightenment might be hired. This would be Washington's gift to his country. What better way to symbolize the new federal nation than with a university sponsored by the republic itself? It was an imaginative and not impractical plan, and yet it remains unrealized more than two centuries later.[1]

It was a vision colored by the college education Washington never had and by the military education he did have. Recalling his years fighting as a young man, Washington especially remembered experiences of community and fraternity—the fraternity of men who fight, sleep, dream, obey, and die together. "A century in the ordinary intercourse, would not have accomplished what the Seven years association in Arms did," he wrote. The new university would similarly offer its students communion—in learning. "Young men from different parts of the United States," he wrote, "would be assembled together and would by degrees discover that here was not that cause for those jealousies and prejudices which one part of the Union had imbibed against another part."[2]

For Washington nothing was more crucial than an educated citizenry. In a free, democratic, representative government that inevitably "gives force to public opinion," Washington wrote, "it is essential that public opinion should be enlightened." The president suggested that newspapers publish congressional debates on all great national issues. He wanted laws to be clear and simple so that average people could comprehend them; he wanted post roads improved so that information about government could circulate fast and reliably.[3]

And yet Washington's many thoughtful efforts to create an educated citizenry ironically confirmed his skepticism about public opinion when it was, in his mind, ill-informed. Already in 1787, he realized that emotion thwarted citizens' rational understanding of the issues. "It is among the evils, and perhaps is not the smallest, of democratical governments," he wrote, "that the people must *feel*, before they will *see*." Toward the end of his second term in office, his wariness about democracy and public opinion had not diminished. "I am *Sure* the Mass of Citizens in these United States *mean well*, and I firmly believe they will always *act well*, whenever they can obtain a *right* understanding of matters." His implication was that public opinion need be taken into account only when it expressed a "right understanding"—something that he conflated with approval of the policies of his own administration.[4]

Washington was not an intolerant man. On the contrary, he counseled "mutual forbearance where there is a difference of opinion." He understood that, in a free government, such differences were unavoidable and people "will express their sentiments, oftentimes imprudently," so allowances must be made for "occasional effervescences." He also recognized that his own judgment, like that of any human, was "very fallible." But he believed that after rational and orderly deliberation had taken place, once local interests and prejudices had been transcended and "accommodations" made, people would find grounds for agreement on the true interest of the nation. And he was convinced that he, as a rational, experienced leader pursuing the public good, had access to that true interest of the nation. "There is but one straight course," he wrote in July 1795, "and that is to seek *truth* and pursue it steadily."[5]

How could a man, who is convinced that his course is that of the "truth," explain opposition to his policies if not as a failure of reason? Even while he himself harbored grave reservations about the Jay Treaty, he wrote that he regretted "exceedingly" that there should have been any difference of opinion on so important a subject. He simply could not imagine that rational and experienced men, after "mature deliberation," might disagree about the public good—and dissent from the policies of his administration. And yet people in a democracy do disagree about major issues—from war and peace to clean water and clean air—and certainly they did in the 1790s. "Are we to establish a political infallibility," one man wrote to a newspaper, "and consecrate a political pope in our country?" But Washington believed so deeply in the power of reason combined with the wisdom of practical experience that he could not accept the idea that no one man or party, especially a minority party like his own, can claim to have privileged or certain insight into the public good. He could not imagine that people might never agree on the public good and that the best they could hope for was a common search for the public good and an open— and contentious—national debate.[6]

The president was hardly oblivious to public opinion. He described himself as "inclined to know the sense of the people upon every matter of great public concern." And as a "servant of the public," he stated that his only wish was "to know the will of my masters, that I may govern myself accordingly." Occasionally, he asked his advisers to learn the sentiments of the people. He requested the help of Jefferson, Madison, and others in drafting parts of his speeches to give them a "more agreeable nature"; and, on major issues like the Jay Treaty, he even gave thought to managing public opinion via the press. "Too much pains," he urged Hamilton, "cannot be taken by those who speak, or write, in favor of the treaty, to place this matter in its true light." He hoped that articles supporting the treaty would be widely disseminated to counteract "the poison" of the opposition.[7]

Despite his repeated statements of interest in public opinion and his efforts to court and even influence it, Washington had little patience for opinion unfavorable to his policies. As far as he was concerned, to reprove the president was to shatter national unity and consensus and subvert constitutional government. His critics, he wrote, "will be satisfied with nothing short of a change in our political system."[8]

The old general bristled when individuals criticized his policies, but when criticism came from organized groups, he considered the situation far more lethal. Political clubs, Washington would contend in 1794, spread their "nefarious doctrines with a view to poison and discontent the minds of the people against the government." These cliques, so many clandestine conspiracies, preferred to meet, he wrote, "under the shade of Night in a conclave."[9]

Washington was referring to the "Democratic-Republican societies." These were political clubs that began to spread throughout the country in the early 1790s, dedicated to promoting and preserving the republican ideals of the Revolution. They were usually passionately pro-French but also concerned with local matters. Through the clubs, citizens from a variety of walks of life—merchants, politicians, landowners, slave owners, professionals, small tradesmen, mechanics, seamen, laborers, and newspaper publishers—participated in political discussions, defining for themselves and their communities the important issues of the day. The editor of the Republican *National Gazette* considered the clubs "absolutely necessary," for without citizens actively engaged in political discussions and debates, "what is every man's business soon becomes no man's business."

In the proliferation of political clubs the president saw a virulent threat to his dream of national unity. The clubs, he wrote, were designed to "sow the seeds of jealousy and distrust among the people" and, if not counteracted, he predicted darkly, would eventually "shake the government to its foundation." Could "anything be more absurd, more arrogant, or more pernicious," he fulminated, than these self-created bodies that presumed to tell a representative government what to do? The clubs, he wrote disparagingly, were tantamount to government by the "Mob." So much for a participatory democracy.[10]

In 1784, a democratic-minded Jefferson had warned Washington—to no avail—that his reputation was being compromised by his association with the Society of the Cincinnati, the elitist organization of revolutionary officers in which membership was hereditary. In 1793, Jefferson issued a not-dissimilar warning to his fellow Virginian, this time against attacking the Democratic-Republican societies. Condemnation of the societies, he explained, would make the president appear as "the head of a party instead of the head of the nation"—and an elitist party, at that. But, in the wake of the Whiskey Rebellion, which Washington considered the product of a conspiracy of admirers of the bloody revolution in France and members of the Democratic Societies, he decided to make a public denunciation of the societies for actions verging on sedition.[11]

This was "perhaps the greatest error of his political life," a despondent James Madison wrote to Monroe. The Federalist "game," in Madison's opinion, was to connect the Democratic-Republican Societies with the Whiskey insurrection, then tie the Republicans in Congress to both, and finally claim that the president stood in opposition to such disorder and subversion. Even worse, Madison saw his cherished Bill of Rights thrown into jeopardy. What could be more "indefensible," he asked, than the president's "arbitrary denunciations" of what the law permits and what the legislature has no right to prohibit? If the government could stifle criticism coming from one lawful source, he continued, it could proceed to suppress criticism from any other, "from the press and from individuals as well as from Societies." Indeed, if it were up to the executive branch alone, no criticism of it would ever be deemed just, Madison held. While the Senate applauded the president's condemnations of the societies, the House refused to follow suit.[12]

In 1794, Madison neatly captured what would be the essence of the repressive Sedition Act, but the dubious distinction of signing that act would fall not to Washington but to his successor, John Adams, in 1798. Though Washington spoke out passionately against factions, even writing that meetings held in opposition to the "constituted authorities" were "*at all times* improper and dangerous," he never took action against them. On the contrary, he believed that "prosecutions" would only make factions grow stronger. The safest route, he felt, was to let them "fall into disesteem." Under Washington's leadership, unlike that of his sanguinary counterparts in France—Robespierre, Saint-Just, and company—there were no political trials and no purges of political adversaries in the United States.[13]

Still, even after the popularity of the Democratic societies waned, Washington continued to decry the Republican opposition. His critics, he railed, were demagogues, foes of order and good government who worked like bees to "distill their poison"; they unfairly attacked the Jay Treaty, enveloping the truth "in mist and false representation." "The cry against the treaty," he wrote, "is like that against a mad-dog; and everyone . . . seems engaged in running it down." And worst of all, Republicans were willing to move "heaven and earth" to help France.[14]

Achingly painful, too, for the aging president were the personal denunciations of him. Newspapers, he complained, attacked him in "indecent terms as could scarcely be applied to a Nero, a notorious defaulter, or even to a common pick-pocket." Every manner of malicious falsehood had been invented to "wound my reputation and feelings." The *Aurora*'s accusation, however, that the president had overdrawn on his annual salary of $25,000 turned out to be correct. Though the infraction had been accidental rather than premeditated, the charges nevertheless caused the president great chagrin. Washington perceived his enemies seeking to reduce his character "as low as they are capable of sinking it, even by resorting to absolute falsehoods." "By god he had rather be in his grave than in his present situation," Jefferson heard him say in 1793. "He had rather be on his farm than to be made emperor of the world, and yet they were charging him with wanting to be a king."[15]

While attacks on Washington were becoming more unreasonable and sharp, Jefferson would come to see the president as the victim of his own popularity, so accustomed to "unlimited applause" that he could "not brook contradiction, or even advice offered unasked." Jefferson's own strategy, he explained to a friend, was to "soothe" and flatter the president and, when he disapproved of his policies, to be silent.[16]

Jefferson was biding his time, waiting for the moment when Republicans could win control of the government and take it back to what they considered the original ideals of the Revolution. And yet Tocqueville would bestow immense praise on the Federalist period, calling it "one of the luckiest circumstances" in American history. The wise and determined leadership of Washington, Hamilton, and others, he wrote, gave the young republic "time to settle down" ("le temps de s'asseoir"). The democratization that would occur under Jefferson, he felt, would have happened sooner or later, but it was the Federalists who created the stable institutions that would later permit the young republic to "face without ill consequences the rapid development of the very doctrines they had opposed."[17]

In July 1796, as Washington stood on the west steps of Mount Vernon, chatting with his guests about a national university, one guest noted a certain moroseness about him. The president had sought relaxation at his Virginia home far away "from the unpleasant scenes which have been, and are continually presenting themselves to my view." He had looked forward to his vacation and to improving his estate. Had his new Windsor chairs arrived, he asked his overseer in early June. Had the green venetian blinds been installed on the west windows? Had cuttings from an apple tree taken hold? Was the slave named Cyrus adjusting to working in the house instead of in the fields?[18]

But even at Mount Vernon, surrounded by fields, trees, friends, and visitors, he could not escape the myriad political problems that required his careful attention. Almost every day he had to respond to a variety of concerns, none of which he considered trivial: American captives in Algiers; clearly demarcated borders to protect the Cherokee lands; Robert Morris's failure to make payments on his contract for lots in the new federal city; a problem with a section of a bill protecting American seamen; the search for a man knowledgeable in casting cannon. Washington even had to scold Secretary of War McHenry, "in a friendly way," for his failure to execute business "promptly and vigorously," and he had to endure the inconvenient and prolonged visit of a dozen members of the Catawba tribe.[19]

More critical, that summer, in the wake of the Jay Treaty, the

French had ratcheted up the level of confrontation. Though the English had not for months seized property on ships bound for France, the Directory government, in July, declared that it would seize English cargo found on American vessels—a policy that would be a major blow to American shipping. The situation, Washington underscored, demanded very serious and cool deliberation. Should a special envoy be sent to France? the president asked both Secretary of State Timothy Pickering and Alexander Hamilton, now his unofficial, trusted adviser. Should the French minister be called in for an explanation? Should the Senate be convened? Was James Monroe, the American minister in France, partly to blame? Washington's cabinet officers accused Monroe of "sinister designs," of making the "notorious enemies" of American government—presumably Republicans and Republican newspaper editors—his own "confidential correspondents." Indeed, Monroe, not disguising his antipathy for the Federalists, refused to defend the Jay Treaty and instead was whipping up French grievances against American policy. Washington decided that Monroe would have to be recalled. It would fall to President Adams to deal with the increasing French spoliation.[20]

At dinner that July day at Mount Vernon, there was little conversation. The host shared a few jokes with the visiting son of the Marquis de Lafayette, young George Washington Lafayette, one guest recalled, and he drank three glasses of wine. Sometimes there were awkward pauses. Still, the president wanted his guests to feel welcome, and one departing visitor commented that "he treated me as if I had lived years in his house with ease and attention." But attacks on him in the press, his failing memory, and even the summer heat were taking their toll. The sixty-four-year-old general was determined to withdraw from public life.[21]

Unlike in 1792, this time no one could persuade him to run for another term. "No consideration under heaven that I can foresee," he wrote in the early summer of 1796, "shall again draw me from the walks of private life." But there was also a reason of principle impelling him to retire: he wanted to give "an early example of rotation" in the nation's highest office. It was a principle, he wrote, that accorded with "the republican spirit" of the Constitution as well as with people's ideas of "liberty and safety." Did he also reason that, if he accepted a third term, he might die in office and the succession of a vice-presidential "heir" might appear monarchical in form? In any case, his retirement would be an astonishing spectacle. What other head of state had turned over power willingly and peacefully to a democratically elected successor? His retirement and the election of 1796 would confirm the mundane but precious timetable of orderly elections every four years—in times of peace as well as war.[22]

The one precedent that Washington set without intending to, though, was that of a two-term limit in the presidency. Hamilton had long objected to such a limitation. In *The Federalist* Number 72, he had forcefully argued that term limits for the chief executive would diminish inducements to good behavior, discourage the president—especially one, like Washington, with a "love of fame"—from undertaking bold new projects, deny the community the advantage of his experience, and preclude political stability. For his part, Washington added that term limits would exclude from the presidency a man whose leadership might be essential in a time of emergency. Washington did not wish to serve more than two terms—out of fatigue, out of a belief in rotation in office, but not out of the principle of term limits. The general, who had, in 1783, strengthened his reputation by resigning from power, was now resigning again, and his departure would strengthen citizens' confidence in the willingness of future presidents similarly to give up power. "Genl. Washington set the example of voluntary retirement after 8. years," President Jefferson would write in 1805, adding, "I shall follow it." The two-term precedent that Washington had never meant to create would hold—until 1940.[23]

In May 1796, Washington had begun making notes for his

Farewell Address, incorporating paragraphs Madison had written for a valedictory in 1792. Then he gave the draft to Hamilton, who revised it, deleting some self-pitying remarks Washington had made about the virulent abuse he had been subjected to; the address should include, Hamilton said, only "such reflections and sentiments as will wear well." Washington implored his friend to insert a section on his wish for a national university, but Hamilton demurred, agreeing only to a general mention of education. Washington gave in but insisted that he would bring the matter before the public "at the closing scene" of his political exit.[24]

After several consultations back and forth, the document was ready. Well, almost ready. At the last minute Washington penned in dozens of small changes. The Farewell Address was never delivered in person but, as Madison had suggested four years earlier, printed in newspapers and in pamphlet form. It came out in September 1796.

The message was powerful: a condemnation of the dual plague of parties and opposition and an attempt to steer the nation back to the president's ideal of unity. And there was foreign policy advice, too.

Washington forcefully portrayed parties as attempting to replace the "delegated will of the nation." They enabled "cunning, ambitious and unprincipled men" to subvert the power of the people and to "usurp for themselves the reins of Government." The ultimate danger of parties, he warned, was that they could provoke such "disorders and miseries" that men would be forced to seek order and security "in the absolute power of an individual," that is, in despotism.

In foreign policy, Washington counseled only temporary alliances with other countries. A nation, he implied, had no permanent allies, only permanent interests. But Washington then went further, weaving his advice on foreign policy into the admonition against parties. For he noted that another dire consequence of parties was that they opened the "door to foreign influence and corruption." Clearly alluding to fiery American partisans of France who had opposed the Jay Treaty, he observed that a foreign country could obtain nefarious influence on American policy through the "channels of party passion." Thus the will of the United States could find itself "subjected to the policy and will" of another country. Originally Washington had used the stronger verb "enslaved" but crossed it out and penned in the verb "subjected" instead.

And what about the individual citizen? Could he responsibly oppose the policies of his government? Perhaps not. Washington used the Farewell Address to remind citizens that their constitutional government was "the offspring of our own choice" and therefore had a "just claim to your confidence and your support." That plea for loyalty to the Constitution was innocuous enough, but Washington then obliterated any distinction between supporting constitutional government and supporting the policies of his administration. "The very idea of the power and the right of the People to establish Government," he wrote, "presupposes the duty of every Individual to *obey* the established Government."

Washington would have explained that his goal was not slavish obedience but, as always, national unity, which was, he wrote, "a main Pillar in the Edifice of your real independence, the support of your tranquillity at home, your peace abroad, of your safety, of your prosperity, of that very Liberty which you so highly prize." But, in Washington's mind, liberty seemed to rest on passive acquiescence.

The locus of Washington's greatest success was also the locus of his greatest failure. In eight years in office, he succeeded brilliantly in fostering *national* unity, but he failed markedly in also trying to foster *political* unity. He mistakenly believed that it was possible to dissolve political differences, forge a national consensus, and banish opposition. He reserved no legitimate space in the political arena for dissidents; and so, ironically, while desiring political unity, he divided Americans into two camps. In one camp he identified friends of his administration; in the other he placed "foes of order and good government." Thus the consequence of his yearning for unity was not harmony but rather polarization and exclusion.[25]

Washington was not a political theorist; he was a political realist, a practical man of formidable experience and wisdom. And yet, despite tumultuous changes in the political terrain, he did not modify his old ideas. "In politics, as in religion, my tenets are few and simple," he wrote in 1795. "The leading one . . . is to be honest and just ourselves, and to exact it from others."[26]

But a truly great leader, a transforming leader, must also be a man of dreams, unafraid to experiment against experience and against the wisdom of the past. He must be not only in step with his times but, as Demosthenes suggested, ahead of them. Perhaps such a leader would have realized that dissent and even opposing visions of the common good nourish a political culture, infusing it with vitality and energy, and that nonviolent political conflict may be healthier for a society than aspirations for unity and harmony.

If Washington was not a prophetic dreamer of a party system that could provide orderly channels for the expression of political opposition, he was hardly alone. After all, the Constitution, as Hamilton had insisted, was created "to unite all parties for the general welfare." Even Thomas Jefferson, the future leader of the Republican opposition, spoke out against parties in 1789. "If I could not go to heaven but with a party," he quipped, "I would not go there at all." Although political parties were evolving in the late eighteenth century, they were shaped more by events than by design, for no one—not Madison, Jefferson, Hamilton, or anyone else—had a theory of party.[27]

And if, after having served as the emblem of national unity, Washington could not suddenly conceive himself as a partisan leader, he was not alone. President Monroe, though a tough party man who would refuse to appoint Federalists to his government, would nevertheless assert that his job was not to be the head of a party but of the nation itself. It would take decades more to learn the lesson that the president could be both.

In the winter of 1796–97, Washington's last months in office, the president could only look forward to his retirement from public life. That winter, again and again, in letters to friends, he repeated that "the curtain is about to close on the political scenes of my life." The old general understood that it was not just the close of a chapter, but the close of a lifetime of public service, from the skirmishes on the Virginia frontier in the 1750s to the presidency of the infant republic in the 1790s. It was not his wish "to mix again in the great world, or to partake in its politics," he wrote to his friends. He portrayed himself as a wearied traveler who sees ahead a "resting place."[28]

In his last message to Congress, Washington surveyed the national and international scenes. There was a new treaty with the Creeks; the English had finally evacuated their northwest posts; Spain and the United States had signed the Treaty of San Lorenzo. Relations with the French were tense, but the president expressed hope that the situation would improve (one member of the audience noticed "extreme agitation" when the president spoke about France). He then advocated the creation of a navy and suggested that the government support the manufacture of key military equipment. Then he turned to agriculture and, noting its "primary importance" to the republic, advised that it should be the "object of public patronage," especially "pecuniary aids to encourage and assist a spirit of discovery and improvement." And he returned to his favorite theme of education, asking Congress once again to establish a national university. And finally the wealthy planter, who had refused a salary as commander of the revolutionary army, now warned against limiting the public sphere to men of private wealth. Calling for fair compensation for all government officers, Washington was urging a meritocracy in which men of modest means would not be excluded from "public trusts."

In his first Inaugural Address, the president had memorably said that "the preservation of the sacred fire of liberty and the destiny of the Republican model of Government are . . . staked on the *experiment* entrusted to the hands of the American people." It was a novel and world-historical political venture, the outcome of which, in 1789, had been uncertain. But eight years later, at the end of his presidency and at the close of his final address to Congress, a satisfied Washington could congratulate his fellow citizens "on the success of the experiment" they had conducted together.

On March 4, Washington arrived alone and on foot at the inauguration of his successor, John Adams, in whose election he had declined to play any role. The nation's father was now a private citizen. During the ceremony, people wept. "It is all grief for the loss of their beloved," Adams carped. Knowing Washington's eagerness to quit the responsibilities of power, Adams imagined Washington saying to himself, "Ay! I am fairly out and you fairly in! See which of us will be happiest." The new vice president, Thomas Jefferson, also considered Washington "fortunate to get off just as the bubble is bursting." The transition was well timed, he wrote Madison, with Washington "leaving others to hold the bag."[29]

While the crowd mournfully bid farewell to Washington, others gloated over his departure. The Republican newspaper *Aurora* rejoiced that "the man who is the source of all the misfortunes of our country is this day reduced to a level with his fellow-citizens, and is no longer possessed of power to multiply evils upon the United States."

Back at Mount Vernon, Washington discovered that his home and his lands were in disarray and in need of much attention and repair. "I find myself in the situation," he confessed, "of a young beginner." Did he remember that, forty-two years earlier, embarking on his journey to the center of the world stage, he had counseled his younger brother to be "serviceable" to the Fairfaxes, for it was in the power of those friends to help them, "as *young beginner's*"? In May 1798, he mentioned to an English friend that the Fairfax estate, Belvoir, was for sale, hoping, perhaps, that the ruins of Belvoir might be restored and the scene of his youth resurrected. That same month he wrote to his first love, Sally Fairfax, who had emigrated with her loyalist family to England before the Revolution. The man who had created a nation now wrote to this elderly widow that not one of the events of his life, "nor all of them together, have been able to eradicate from my mind the recollection of those happy moments, the happiest in my life, which I have enjoyed in your company." Then, an invitation. "I have wondered often," he wrote, "that you should not prefer spending the evening of your life" in Virginia with him and her other old friends. At the age of sixty-six, Washington was ready to be a young beginner again.[30]

But politically he would change in retirement. The idealistic president, who had wanted the United States to be a place of asylum for "the poor, the needy, and the oppressed of the Earth," in 1798 endorsed the Alien Act authorizing the president to deport foreigners regarded as dangerous. He now viewed immigrants as a potentially conspiratorial fifth column, sent to America "for the *express purpose* of poisoning the minds of our people" and alienating them from the "government of their choice." And the president who had been the target of a virulent press but had moderately counseled against reprisals, also endorsed the Sedition Act, passing along to his friends the judicial opinion that upheld it and remarking that, if the charges against one editor were true, "punishment ought to be inflicted."[31]

Events were hardening Washington's Federalist convictions. The man who had repudiated the very notion of political factions came to see that there was no circumventing political reality.

When he surprisingly agreed to reenter public life in 1798 and serve as commander in chief of the army, in anticipation of war with France (ordering "cockades and stars" for the epaulettes of his uniform), Washington insisted that army officers be Federalists in whom he could have complete confidence. He wanted no one who displayed "general opposition" to the government or "predilection to French measures."[32]

As company Washington enjoyed "good Federal characters" for whom the "best dessert" was anti-Republican cuisine. And when his friends asked him in 1799 to run again for the presidency in 1800, his sharp awareness of party—not the idea of rotation in office or term limits—colored his reasons for declining. Sadly, it had become impossible, he remarked, to be a national leader. "I am thoroughly convinced," he wrote, "I should not draw a single vote from the anti-federal side." He explained that his Republican opponents could choose as their candidate "a broomstick," but if the broomstick were called a "true son of Liberty," it would command "their votes in toto!"[33]

The dark menace of parties also disposed the president to lend credence to a variety of conspiracy theories circulating among Federalists. He entertained the bizarre notion that a sect of upper-class European mystics, the "Illuminati," wanted to take over the United States—along with the rest of the world. It was "too evident to be questioned," he wrote, that the "diabolical tenets" of the Illuminati had infected American society through the medium of the Democratic societies.[34]

Still, there were limits to Washington's openness to Federalist conspiracy theories. Under "the influence or coercion of France," Hamilton informed Washington in 1798, Republicans wanted to remodel the Constitution, with Jefferson and his cronies determined "to make this country a province of France." That would have been interesting work for the author of the Declaration of Independence. Washington replied that, while Republicans might want to subvert the Constitution, it was not out of loyalty to

France. Republicans had "no more regard for [France]," he wrote to Lafayette, "than for the Grand Turk."[35]

When Federalists implored Washington to try to prevent President Adams from sending a minister to negotiate with the Directory government in Paris and end the quasi war with France, a sage Washington declined to intervene. "The vessel is afloat or very nearly so," he wrote in November 1799, one month before he died. "Considering myself as a passenger only, I shall trust to the mariners whose duty it is to watch, to steer it into a safe port."[36]

The vessel, his legacy, would remain intact.

9

Collective Leadership: Remaking the Constitution

The most momentous aspect of the American Revolution was what did not happen. Revolutions before and since in Europe and Latin America would erupt in ferocious conflict as a victorious faction of insurrectionists seized power and crushed the opposition. That is what did not happen under the leadership of George Washington.

Why the exception? In part because Washington shifted creatively from role to role—from Virginia planter to revolutionary generalissimo to remaker of the founding Constitution as he led the new government; with no rival who could dent his awesome reputation, he avoided the rigidity that invites extreme opposition. In even greater part because he not only adapted to the ever-changing political environment but altered that environment as he shifted from role to role. Thus he shed his military command before his critics could accuse him of lusting for power. He influenced the Constitutional Convention not by giving speeches but simply by *being* there—by offering a dominating presence, by expressing his views in off-hours chats with fellow delegates, by embodying a form of leadership that the convention could not ignore, and eventually by opening the power of the executive to vast expansion.

In the end, Washington's presidency became a kind of continuing constitutional convention as he built almost unimpeded power into the executive branch. He not only occupied the office, he virtually conquered it: he became president before there was a presidency. His surefootedness failed him only toward the end, when the political environment changed once again and left him facing storms he could not dispel or even fully comprehend.

As chief executive, he exerted administrative leadership early in his presidency. He established in effect a cabinet that had no standing in the Constitution. He developed informal but explicit priorities and provided policy leadership to his top officers—Hamilton, Jefferson, and others. His rising authority spilled over into Congress, as the chief executive became in effect chief legislator. While he vetoed few congressional measures, he did not need to, for Congress was in no mood to impede the hero-president. Under the checks and balances system, he could thwart or ignore or follow Congress, in contrast to political leaders abroad who were at least nominally responsible to their parliaments. Typically, he did not so much ignore Congress as govern through it.

But his was by no means a one-man presidency. It would rank later as embodying a collective leadership never to be surpassed in American presidential history. Collegiality, of course, was relatively easy among a small team of men who had worked closely together through the revolutionary and founding eras. But his colleagues were leaders in their own right, with their own philosophies and policies passionately embraced.

In part, this collectivity was based on sheer need, as Washington turned for advice to the men of his cabinet—especially Hamilton—who had special expertise. Critics charged that he was unduly dependent on his cabinet members and others—that they even wrote many of his key letters and speeches. The critics were correct but shortsighted. Washington had such faith in his advisers' competence and creativity that he could safely appropriate their best ideas and rhetoric. Besides, one could make the same defense of Washington's "theft of words" that later biographers would offer of Franklin D. Roosevelt's speeches: Who, after all, had selected the wordsmiths?

The Washington administration's collective leadership reflected a more pervasive force—the basic unity of the revolutionary and founding generations. "The core revolutionary principle in this view is collective rather than individualistic," historian Joseph J. Ellis wrote, "for it sees the true spirit of '76 as the virtuous surrender of personal, state, and sectional interests to the larger purposes of American nationhood, first embodied in the Continental Army and later in the newly established federal government." And this collectivity characterized as well the internal relationships in the Washington presidency to a marked degree. Unity under Washington would have lasting implications—positive ones for national development but potentially negative ones for individual rights.[1]

Washington's collective leadership also reflected the enormous respect, despite their sharp differences, that the teammates had for one another's talents—the cabinet for Washington's character and convictions, the cabinet members for one another, and Washington's dependence on his colleagues' intellectual power and creativity. The president could not forget that Adams, Jefferson, and Madison, among others, were highly educated men, while he had had to learn from experience and from reading on his own. So he would listen to them, debate with them, and often go along with them—but always he would subject their ideas and proposals to the demanding standard based on his own long immersion in the school of political hard knocks.

During the shaping of the new government, all eyes fastened on the president—the chief executive and chief magistrate—but fewer on the politician-legislators in the first Congress. It was supremely ironic, two years after the Constitutional Convention that established Congress as the central authority of the new republic, that the national legislature seemed far less visible to the populace than the hero in the executive office. Twenty-six senators and several dozen congressmen were busy debating and legislating while the president—especially with the help of Hamilton's economic proposals—dominated the policy-making process.

Also ironic was the posture of a young congressman from Virginia, James Madison, who had aspired to the Senate but had to settle for election to the "lower" chamber. The author of *The Federalist* Number 10, the most brilliant exposition of checks and balances ever written, Madison was hardly checking the president. He was advising Washington, and he even authored his first message to Congress. For a year or two Washington relied on him for information and advice about congressional doings. It can be argued that Madison was not betraying his own constitutional principles. On the contrary, his theory of the separation of powers was actually a theory of the separation of *institutions* that still required the intermingling of politicians who have different and conflicting constituencies. But few argued theory when they beheld the ambitious young Virginian busy in the executive councils.

Nothing more tellingly reflected Washington's innovative leadership than Madison's supportive role in Congress during the first year of the administration. Madison—the celebrated advocate of the separation of powers—now serving as "the President's man" in the national legislature! One historian has called him a "virtual prime minister," though others might nominate Hamilton for that imaginary post. Neither Washington nor Madison seemed to make much of the unlikely relationship. Indeed, it was probably the first example of what political scientist Fred I. Greenstein has called "hidden-hand leadership"—the ability to wield influence so discreetly through others as to minimize opposition.[2]

The Republican press, however, castigated a leadership that had apparently abandoned constitutional checks and balances. We can pause today to ask, What if the advocates of a radical separation of powers had had their way, leaving basic lawmaking and policy making exclusively in the hands of Congress? What if the Framers had established a plural executive or had otherwise weakened the office in 1787? Would not a rigid system of setting power against power have proved even more inadequate in confronting the dire crises of the 1790s than the Articles of Confederation had been in coping with the pressures of the 1780s?

If a weak national government had imploded, it probably would have been during a crisis over foreign or military policy, such as the Jay Treaty controversy had been, for the treaty polarized people ideologically and politically and triggered an outpouring of popular anger. When word leaked out about the treaty, it was "like an electric velocity to every part of the Union," Madison said. Both he and Jefferson turned against what Jefferson called an infamous treaty. The fact that the moderate, soft-spoken Madison could bitterly blame passage of the treaty on "the exertions and influence of Aristocracy, Anglicism, and mercantilism" reveals the depth of the discord the treaty provoked. But the new republic was able to absorb and contain this conflict without imploding—thanks to Washington's backing of the treaty buttressed by his political skill and enormous prestige. Conflict was defanged—if not eliminated.[3]

Still, a historical meditation on Washington's use of presidential power cannot focus alone on what was necessary and expedient for his own political situation. The first chief executive was creating precedents that would be greedily seized on and invoked by future presidents, competing parties, and members of Congress for decades to come. His strategy of government would be imitated or assailed by political leaders of the future just as his idea of no "entangling alliances" would be exploited by isolationists in future crisis situations. The Constitution had been written for all time, not merely for the first occupant of the presidency. Should Washington have had posterity more in mind as he was taking on such a dominant role in foreign policy making?

Only if he believed he was violating the Constitution—but he most decidedly did not so believe. To him, the Constitution was more a grant of power than a curb on it. The presidential role must not only be to administer—it must be executive and even legislative. He wanted to work with Congress and not be separated from it. He even proposed a special chamber apart from both the executive offices and the halls of Congress as a place for senators and the president to agree on policy. Sketching out his ideas for government buildings in the new federal city, he wrote, "Whenever the Government shall have buildings of its own, an executive Chamber will no doubt be provided, where the Senate will generally attend the president." The plan got nowhere.[4]

"His consensus style of leadership," according to political scientist Glenn Phelps, "was evidence of his concern for energetic government. Like many of the 'nationalists' of the Revolutionary War, he remembered the fragmentation of congressional power into numerous boards and committees, each guarding its prerogatives jealously. Washington wanted the new constitutional government to speak and act as much as possible with one voice. . . . Whether deliberate or not, Washington's grand plan bore a strong resemblance to the King-and-council form of the British parliamentary system." No wonder good republicans were furious.[5]

So furious they threw back at him any ammunition they could find. If he wanted to interpret the general terms of the Constitution in his own way, they cried, what about *The Federalist* (which Washington had dutifully read) that established the separation of powers and checks and balances in authoritative detail. The president would have none of this. He saw *The Federalist*—written by Hamilton as well as by Madison—less as a restrictive argument than as a springboard for "energy in the executive." Modern reinterpretations of *The Federalist* have given considerable credence to Washington's view.[6]

That view would echo down through the chambers of American history—to Lincoln's use of his war power and Theodore

Roosevelt's exploitation of his executive authority, to Woodrow Wilson's and Franklin D. Roosevelt's extension of their foreign policy-making powers on the world scene, to Lyndon B. Johnson's and Richard M. Nixon's war making in Vietnam, to the intrusions of both Presidents Bush in the Middle East. George Washington might have disagreed with the specific policies and actions—but not with the "energy in the executive" supporting them.

Washington viewed himself as president of all the people, as a leader rising above factional disputes and ideological divisions. Hence he was mystified as well as mortified by the conflicts that erupted as the election of 1792 neared. Even though he would be unopposed, he sensed grievances among the people. Had he not been evenhanded in his choice of cabinet members and other officials of the new government? In his appointments, hadn't he carefully balanced friends of Jefferson and friends of Hamilton? Hadn't he preached over and over again about the need for unity as the foundation of the new republic? But he heard the rumblings of discontent from a variety of sources, from within his own cabinet and especially from the dozen journals he subscribed to. During his second term, the rumblings turned into a cacophony of shrill attacks.

What caused the rifts in the united support for the president? Some contemporaries said Hamilton's economic program, which stirred latent antipathy to the pro-mercantile, pro-capitalistic, urban, upper-class Americans who would gain most from it. Some said the Jay Treaty, which unleashed passionate opposition from Francophiles. Historically the split went further back—to the radical countrymen and cobblestone rebels who had fought most fiercely against the Tories, to the supporters of the Articles of Confederation who feared "monarchical rule" in America, to the vociferous critics of the "centralization" and "tyranny" inherent in the new Constitution. It was a rupture waiting to happen. But it would not happen under Washington. He would have been astonished—

though he never would have admitted it—if any serious candidate had opposed him in 1792. Of course, none did—it was one thing to run against a Federalist, something quite different to take on an icon, a hero-president, already the Father of his Country.

Given the fact that electoral opposition to Washington was feeble, why did he react so angrily to the party and factional and individual criticism that assailed him? How could this self-confident, resolute, firmly established man erupt in fury against the "poisonous" critics and conspiratorial factions, as he envisaged them? It was in part a rational reaction. He suspected—rightly in some cases—that hostile nations sought to foster dissent and even separatism in his own nation. Less rationally, perhaps, the boundless adulation of his countrymen had inevitably given him the heady feeling that he did indeed speak for all the people, that he was not unlike a monarch who might make mistakes but who must be supported on the assumption that—for the sake of the security of the country—"the king can do no wrong." All this related to Washington's boundless concern for his reputation.

Still, Washington was no innocent about the inevitability of dissension in a new republic or any other country. He was long used to conflict among France and Britain and other powers, between American settlers and Indians, between rival politicians in Virginia, and between southern slaveholders and northern abolitionists in the slowly developing fissure over slavery. He had followed parliamentary battles in Britain that continued decade after decade and were taken for granted. With his own often uncontrollable temper, he knew that humankind was naturally contentious, as philosophers had long observed. But he transcended those day-to-day quarrels by adhering to a powerful, overriding conviction.

That conviction was a belief in unity that undergirded his ultimate value of order. It was the kind of unity that embodied more than everyday cooperation and harmony among people. It was the idea of a broad and deep consensus so grounded and so powerful that no divisive force could stand against it—indeed such a force would be swallowed up in it. In embracing this doctrine, Washington was anticipating, even prefacing, one of the most potent and persistent ideas in American presidential history—the notion of an adjournment of politics, the idea that a political leader can rise above party and create a plebiscitary presidency that would represent all the people by promoting consensus. Presidents after Washington, waging bitter combat and asking for a suspension of politics, did not have to argue their case—they could simply invoke memories of the first president who so transcended politics that no one ever ran against him or even voted against him. A suspension of politics would be especially popular in the face of real or perceived threats from abroad.

And the idea has persisted for two centuries after Washington's presidency. In 2003, a candidate for the top job pledged that as chief executive he would raise the nation "above partisan politics" and "put the country first." The more partisan a politician is in seeking office, it seems, the more he claims to rise above party politics. George Washington lives![7]

Open conflict is inevitable in a democracy; the question is what form it takes, how it is organized or disorganized. In the early American republic, conflict might have taken any one of diverse forms. It might have degenerated into a war between northern and southern states—as indeed it did sixty years later. The Articles of Confederation might have led to permanent conflict among states. Conflict might have taken the form of a centralized authoritarian dictatorship arrayed against most of the populace. Or it might have become a relatively benign and stable battle between parties—perhaps only two parties.

The Washington presidency, however, bequeathed an enduring conflict far more complex than a simple Federalist-Republican or conservative-liberal dichotomy; rather it spawned what can be called the Washingtonian/Hamiltonian, Madisonian, and Jeffersonian models of government under the Constitution. The Washingtonian/Hamiltonian model was one of vigorous executive leadership, a flexible and resourceful administration, presidential rather than party leadership—a model that overrode the checks and balances without blatantly violating the spirit of the Constitution but that threatened to pulverize the opposition. The Madisonian model was brilliantly articulated by the Virginia philosopher-politician, the author of *The Federalist* Number 10 and Number 51. Although Madison violated his own theory by aiding and advising Washington early in his presidency, he and his political allies exploited his checks and balances ideas in calling for minority rights, limited government, and severe restraints on presidential power. The Jeffersonian model was the product less of grand theory than of populist pressures generated by grassroots groups and by politicians hostile to Hamilton's Federalist policies. If the Washingtonian/Hamiltonian model implied a federal government revolving around an energetic president, and if the Madisonian model implied a prudent, less daring and less active president, with powers balanced between the legislative and executive forces, the Jeffersonian model was of almost revolutionary potential, implying government by majority rule, under strong presidential leadership with a highly competitive two-party system and a more popular democratic and egalitarian impetus than either of the two other models.[8]

Hamilton, cut down by Aaron Burr's bullet, would never have the opportunity to carry out his and Washington's presidential strategy. Jefferson followed his own strategy in breaking with Washington, building an opposition party, taking it to victory in 1800, and governing as a party leader. Madison as president would try to shape his government in the true spirit of checks and balances, but his plans soon fell victim to centrifugal forces in his administration. He discovered that if he did not exert force through governmental channels, his opponents would exert force through those same circuits against him. He learned that political structures could never be neutral, and that even checks and balances, carefully designed for fairness to all, favored some policies and interests against others. The net effect for Madison was a weakened presidency.

What were the implications during the nineteenth and twentieth centuries of the Washingtonian/Hamiltonian, Jeffersonian, and Madisonian strategies of leadership and government? Each model was subject to distortion and caricature. The extremes of the Washingtonian/Hamiltonian model—opportunism, manipulation, presidential pressuring—raised formidable threats of excessive presidential power, as in the cases of Lyndon B. Johnson and George W. Bush, and would arouse intense fears as the republic entered its third century. The Democratic Party's use of patronage under Jackson and other presidents was Jeffersonian party government carried to extremes. The Madisonian model was easily caricatured by Senator John Calhoun's theory of "concurrent majority rule," proposed while the issue of slavery was intensifying. Calhoun, who would become a leading secessionist, favored not straight majority rule but a "supermajority rule" that granted any substantial region or interest the power to veto acts of Congress.[9]

How strong a leader was George Washington? How effective was his model of presidential leadership? Did he produce substantial and lasting changes in the life of the nation and the liberty and happiness of its people? Some presidential scholars see Washington as essentially a symbolic leader who kept the nation united during perilous times. Others consider him mainly a "facilitator," much constrained in a political context hostile to strong presidential leadership. Still others view Washington as actually living up to the classic picture of him as a great president, a strong leader, indeed, the Founder.[10]

The evaluation of Washington's presidency depends in large part on whether we assess him as an individual leader or as the central figure in a *collective* leadership system, the presidency. As an individual leader dealing with his cabinet, with Congress, and with the public, Washington was at most a skillful transactional politician, a negotiator, a political broker, yes, a facilitator. Given his aloof bearing and his distaste for political brokerage, he was surprisingly adept at the give-and-take of presidential-congressional politics. Where his formal authority such as the veto power was inadequate, he marshaled authority in ways that would become customary for future presidents—using his patronage power to appoint good Federalists, pressuring the Senate, negotiating treaties with foreign powers, communicating in a variety of ways with individual members of Congress. These activities could produce needed changes but not dramatic transformations.

It was as head of a large collective leadership, the presidency, that Washington became a transforming leader. If Hamilton principally authored his economic program, he did so as Washington's appointee and with the president's strong support. If Washington converted the presidency from a mere array of officers and formal responsibilities laid out in the Constitution into a near monarchy, it was because of the teamwork Washington insisted on and the caliber of his team. His team had legs—that is, the members of the predominantly Federalist Congress and the hundreds of state and local politicians who embraced the president's cause. Thus, his greatest act of governmental change was the enlargement of the presidency, bequeathing to future leaders a potentially powerful office. And he set high standards for the running of that office.

The first test of transforming leadership is the capacity to bring about comprehensive, intended, and lasting change. In his creation of a strong presidency, in his initiation of major economic and other measures, in his nationalistic foreign policy making, Washington brought about fundamental alterations in the structure as well as in the role of government. While his austere type of leadership would rarely be imitated by future presidents, his empowerment of the presidency through the fashioning of a collective leadership created precedents that would enable future presidents to forge continuing and lasting changes. Some of the political alterations he brought about were intentional, such as a strong Federalist presidency; wholly unintended, however, was the rise of a rival party that would disrupt the politics of unity and consensus that he prized so much. Of all these changes, his reshaping of the constitutional balance of powers—in effect, his remaking of the Constitution—would have the most impact on the developing republic.

But in the longer run, Washington's transforming leadership would have to meet a test even more exacting than that of lasting change—the fundamental test of moral values.

Epilogue:
Moral Leadership:
The Mixed Legacy

If a New York or Philadelphia newsman had accosted Washington as he stepped out of his gilded carriage—an unlikely happening—and asked him, "What is the single most crucial quality of a great leader?" and if Washington had deigned to reply—even more unlikely—his answer probably would have been *"Character!"* What would he have meant by this compelling but vague word?

As a young man he had been most explicit—character consisted of polite and virtuous social behavior. Some of the virtues he absorbed from the *Rules of Civility*—"Eat not in the Streets"; "In your Apparel be Modest"—come through to us today as etiquette book niceties or as advice to a young man on the make. But other maxims taught the importance of empathy and responsibility. "When you see a Crime punished, you may be inwardly Pleased, but always shew Pity to the Suffering Offender"; "Let your Conversation be without Malice or Envy"; "Undertake not what you cannot Perform." On the level of these virtues, the young Washington acted well.

But Washington the acquisitive planter, entrepreneur, and president would later be put to the more exigent test of ethics and integrity, and here he did not always pass with flying colors. Coldly interested in his own profits, canny and competitive in his financial dealings, he appropriated for himself the best land from the acreage set aside for veterans of the army of 1754 and, through his brother, convinced some of the men to sell their shares to him, as historian John Ferling remarked, "for a pittance." When one veteran complained, the hot-tempered Washington exploded, berating the man for his "stupidity and sottishness." As president, he would push for the new federal city to be located on the Potomac, in which he had business interests, and near Alexandria, where he owned real estate. So sterling was Washington's public reputation that one is tempted to welcome such signs of human fallibility—perhaps even to hope that John Adams was justified in complaining that when the retiring president was selling off possessions, he tried to fob off on him, for $2,000, two old nags.[1]

If Washington had remained a plantation owner or simply a private citizen, he would have been judged by the ethical standards of his community. But as the most illustrious public man of his time, he would be measured by higher and broader criteria than either virtues or business ethics. He would be judged by the reigning moral principles of his time, by the values that buttressed the entire republican project of his young nation. From the start, American leaders would be evaluated not only for their private conduct and personal honesty but also for their commitment to values of national security, individual liberty, equality, and the welfare of the people, unforgettably summarized in the Declaration of Independence as life, liberty, and the pursuit of happiness. How to define these values, how to prioritize them, how to apply them would be at the heart of debates over presidential leadership beginning with Washington and lasting at least two centuries.

These were Enlightenment values, examined in depth by Hutcheson and Ferguson in Scotland and by Rousseau and Voltaire in France, in turn distilled into noble utterances by Jefferson and Madison and Washington himself. Washington had read little of the philosophers, but he had absorbed much from thinkers he admired and from the great debates of the era. And he had a strong sense of priorities among the Enlightenment's ideals.

For him, security, stability, order—the nation's ability to survive, that is, its very *life*—constituted the supreme value, because the other high principles could not be established and expanded except in an environment free from fear and tumult. He had come too close to disunity and defeat in the Valley Forge winter to doubt the importance of the sheer survival of his country. How could liberty, for example, be protected amid the kind of internecine conflict he witnessed from afar in the French Revolution? How could order survive if rebels and dissidents were allowed to run riot?

Like any good student of the Enlightenment, he believed in liberty, but only to a limited degree. Certainly he supported freedom of religious belief and expression; he made conciliatory statements about faiths other than his own, those of Catholics, Jews, even "Mohametans." But the supreme test of Enlightenment values in this era—dominated by absolutist regimes—was *political* liberty, which he formally extolled as indispensable in a republic but which he deserted in the political crucible. The test came after his presidency—when he had the good fortune to deal with it at a distance—in his support for the Federalists' Alien and Sedition Acts. The fact that, as an ex-president, he was not under any political pressure offers a good test of his real feelings—his willingness to subordinate the supreme Enlightenment belief in individual liberty to what he saw as the overwhelming need for national security. Washington's personal and political security in 1798, along with his learning experiences as revolutionary leader and president, might have moderated his apprehension of subversion, opposition, and dissension. They did not.

The issue was not only freedom from excessive government restriction but a broader and more expansive value—the right to happiness. For a man who rejected sentimentalism, it was remarkable how often Washington used the word "happiness." His adherence to the Enlightenment definition of happiness as *public* happiness, founded in reason, as a human responsibility rather than mere personal enjoyment, ultimately as fulfillment of a moral responsibility to the nation as well as to others—all this strikes the virtuous citizen of today as a fine recipe for good leadership and followership. Washington's derogation of happiness as sheer self-gratification and pleasure seeking sharpens our concern that too many Americans in the twenty-first century see happiness as *only* that.

Yet Washington's idea of happiness was so elevated that he seemed to overlook the fact that to millions of his fellow Americans it appeared esoteric and even elitist, for they found happiness in the comfort of a decent habitation, in the pleasures of material satisfactions, in the pursuit of everyday enjoyments, and in a good income—forms of happiness that he recognized but placed second to public happiness. Ultimately Washington's "Federalist" conception of happiness would play politically into the hands of Jeffersonian Republicans, who would offer people what they wanted—a more earthy, material kind of happiness—and who would hence benefit at the polls.

Nothing could have more bluntly challenged Washington's view of happiness than slavery. To move from his public world of civility and decorum, statesmanship and diplomacy, revolutionary leadership and constitution making to his private world at Mount Vernon is to descend into a southern plantation of several thousand acres, two hundred slaves managed by hard-driving overseers, directed from near or afar by entrepreneurs busy computing profit and loss, sales and expenses, the buying and selling of slaves as chattel property. Washington was the unchallenged master of these slaves, yet utterly dependent on them, in a hierarchical community. The slaves, adults and children, as historian Fritz Hirschfeld noted, "plowed the fields, tended the crops, harvested the wheat and corn, dried the tobacco, cured the hams, picked the apples, built the barns, mended the fences, milked the cows, collected the eggs, operated the distillery, fished the Potomac, drained the swamps, herded the cattle, sheared the sheep, loaded the cargoes, and carried out the other menial tasks associated with the upkeep and operation of a large and mainly self-sufficient plantation—and it was the profit from their toil that resulted in the creation of the luxury and great beauty . . . that made Washington's ancestral home a magnificent showplace during much of his lifetime." These were precisely the menial tasks of millions of Washington's fellow white citizens—but they enjoyed, to an increasing degree, the blessings of liberty.

One could fantasize that Washington and his slaves might have been bound together as leader and followers. But in reality he was their ruler, not their leader; he would not have dreamed of mobilizing them politically, as leaders may do, and his slaves would not have dared to burst out of bondage and lead him, as followers may do. His plantation was not a little democracy.

And yet in private Washington increasingly opposed slavery. His disapproval intensified as he accepted blacks as soldiers in the revolutionary army, as he met antislavery Britishers and corresponded with other enlightened men such as his friend Lafayette who wanted to see an end to slavery, and as he read the Philadelphia press. And he was most eloquent and revealing about his true beliefs in his private correspondence. As early as 1786 he expressed to a business acquaintance his hope that "slavery in this Country may be abolished by slow, sure, and imperceptible degrees."[2]

But in public Washington was silent about slavery. Why was this courageous and comprehending man so timid to speak out in public about his changing views? He possessed the benevolence—and concern for his eternal reputation—to free his slaves upon his death, or upon Martha's death, should she outlive him; but during his lifetime he made no public pronouncements against slavery.

Not because he was any kind of racist or Negrophobe, as some critics claimed. Rather because he believed that a public stand in favor of abolition would endanger the value he prized above all: unity grounded in order, the stability and survival of the nation. When the House of Representatives voted in 1790 that the federal government had no jurisdiction over ending the slave trade or emancipation, Washington voiced approval that the issue had "at length been put to sleep." Discussions of slavery, he judged, had been "mal-apropos." More important to the survival of the young republic, he felt, was "a spirit of accommodation." Doubtless he had an intuition, perhaps more, of the terrifying potential for conflict that slavery portended, indeed, conflict that one day would rupture the union. But liberty and happiness, buttressed by justice and equality, were not only lesser values than order for Washington but were dependent upon order.[3]

Yet Washington could hardly imagine that the reverse was true, that ultimately order and stability are dependent on those "lesser" values, because, without them, order deteriorates into despotism and tyranny. It would take more historical imagination than even Washington possessed to understand that a proper balance among the three values of life, liberty, and the pursuit of happiness could have produced steady compromises that might have achieved emancipation before the bloody conflict of the 1860s. But such an outcome would have required a combination of transforming and transactional leadership that the fragmented constitutional system could not support. Washington wanted all three of the great American values, but he did not work out the interrelationship among them. It would remain for other leaders to do this—most notably Franklin D. Roosevelt in his "Four Freedoms."

Ultimately, then, what was the legacy of Washington's leadership and especially of his presidency? It was an array of great initiatives in establishing a strong executive and in formulating innovative economic policies of lasting import. It was a successful experiment in collective leadership composed of the brilliant cabinet members Washington chose and whom he empowered to try to overcome the fragmented government. It was a politics of mobilizing people behind his Federalist policies and his Federalist allies but also a politics of failing to anticipate the vital need for an opposition party pledged to offer an alternative route to the people's liberty and happiness.

Transcending all this was the legacy for all Americans of Washington the *man*—the revolutionary hero, the founding president, the First Citizen of the young republic.

Sources and Notes

SOURCES

AJL *The Adams-Jefferson Letters.* Ed. Lester J. Cappon. Chapel Hill: University of North Carolina Press, 1959, 2 vols.

DA Adair, Douglass. *Fame and the Founding Fathers.* Ed. Trevor Colbourn. New York: W. W. Norton, 1974.

DGW *The Diaries of George Washington.* Ed. Donald Jackson and Dorothy Twohig. Charlottesville: University Press of Virginia, 1976–.

EM Elkins, Stanley, and Eric McKitrick. *The Age of Federalism.* New York: Oxford University Press, 1993.

F Freeman, Douglas S. *George Washington.* New York: Charles Scribner's Sons, 1948–1957, 7 vols.; 7th vol. by John Carroll and Mary Ashworth.

FA Ames, Fisher. *Works.* Ed. Seth Ames. Boston: Little, Brown, and Company, 1854.

FB Ellis, Joseph J. *Founding Brothers: The Revolutionary Generation.* New York: Alfred A. Knopf, 2000.

FG Ferling, John E. *The First of Men: A Life of George Washington.* Knoxville: University of Tennessee Press, 1988.

FL Flexner, James Thomas. *George Washington.* Boston: Little, Brown, and Company, 1965–1972, 4 vols.

GF Washington, George. *Writings.* Ed. W. C. Ford. New York: G. P. Putnam's Sons, 1889–1893, 14 vols.

GM Morris, Gouverneur. *Diary and Letters.* Ed. Anne C. Morris. New York: Charles Scribner's Sons, 1888, 2 vols.

GPC Phelps, Glenn. "George Washington: Precedent Setter." In Thomas E. Cronin, ed., *Inventing the American Presidency.* Lawrence: University Press of Kansas, 1989, 259–81.

GW Washington, George. *Writings.* Ed. John C. Fitzpatrick. Washington, D.C.: United States Government Printing Office, 1931–1944, 39 vols.

HS Hamilton, Alexander. *Papers.* Ed. Harold C. Syrett. New York: Columbia University Press, 1961–1987, 27 vols.

JAW *Letters of John Adams Addressed to his Wife.* Ed. C. F. Adams. Boston: Little, Brown, and Company, 1841.

JF Jefferson, Thomas. *Writings.* Ed. Paul Leicester Ford. New York: G. P. Putnam's Sons, 1892–1899, 10 vols.

JMS Smith, James Morton. *The Republic of Letters: The Correspondence Between Thomas Jefferson and James Madison 1776–1826.* New York: W. W. Norton, 1995, 3 vols.

JNR Rakove, Jack N. *The Beginnings of National Politics: An Interpretive History of the Continental Congress.* New York: Alfred A. Knopf, 1979.

LDW White, Leonard D. *The Federalists: A Study in Administrative History.* New York: Macmillan, 1948.

LLF Weaver, David R. "Leadership, Locke, and the Federalist." *American Journal of Political Science* 41, no. 2 (April 1997): 420–46.

MAS Schwartz, Barry. *George Washington: The Making of an American Symbol.* New York: Free Press, 1987.

MG Morgan, Edmund S. *The Genius of George Washington.* New York: W. W. Norton, 1980.

PG Burns, James MacGregor. *Presidential Government.* Boston: Houghton Mifflin, 1966.

PJM Madison, James. *Papers.* Ed. William Hutchinson, Robert Rutland et al. Charlottesville: University Press of Virginia 1962–.

PTJ Jefferson, Thomas. *Papers.* Ed. Julian Boyd. Princeton: Princeton University Press, 1950–.

PWJA Carey, George W., ed. *The Political Writings of John Adams.* Washington, D.C.: Regnery Publishing, 2000.

RFC *The Records of the Federal Convention of 1787.* Ed. Max Farrand. New Haven: Yale University Press, 1966, 4 vols.

SIP Schlesinger, Arthur M., Jr. *The Imperial Presidency.* Boston: Houghton Mifflin, 1973.

SL Leibiger, Stuart. *Founding Friendship: George Washington, James Madison, and the Creation of the American Republic.* Charlottesville: University Press of Virginia, 1999.

SR Buel, Richard. *Securing the Revolution: Ideology in American Politics, 1789–1815.* Ithaca, N.Y.: Cornell University Press, 1972.

TDA Tocqueville, Alexis de. *De la Démocratie en Amérique* [1840]. Paris: Garnier-Flammarion, 1981.

WAC Phelps, Glenn. *George Washington and American Constitutionalism.* Lawrence: University Press of Kansas, 1993.

WAS Wood, Gordon S. "George Washington on the Abolition of Slavery." *New York Journal of American History* 65 (Spring 2003), 39–42.

WBC Phelps, Glenn. "George Washington and the Building of the Constitution." *Congress and the Presidency* 12, no. 2 (Autumn 1985).

WC Wills, Garry. *Cincinnatus: George Washington and the Enlightenment.* Garden City, N.Y.: Doubleday and Company, 1984.

WJA Adams, John. *Works.* Ed. Charles Francis Adams. Boston: Little, Brown, and Company, 1850–1856, 10 vols.

WJM Madison, James. *Writings.* Ed. Gaillard Hunt. New York: G. P. Putnam's Sons, 1900–1910, 9 vols.

WLC Edwards, George C. "George Washington's Leadership of Congress: Director or Facilitator?" *Congress and the Presidency* 18, no. 2 (Autumn 1991): 163–80.

WR Washington, George. *Writings.* Ed. John Rhodehamel. New York: Library of America, 1997.

WRL Boller, Paul F. "George Washington and Religious Liberty." *William and Mary Quarterly,* Third Series, 17, no. 4 (October 1960): 486–506.

WS Hirschfeld, Fritz. *George Washington and Slavery: A Documentary Portrayal.* Columbia: University of Missouri Press, 1997.

VL Burns, James MacGregor. *The Vineyard of Liberty.* New York: Vintage, 1982.

PROLOGUE

1. VL, 64–66.
2. GW, 30:251–52.
3. GW, 30:268.
4. GW, 28:7.

1: FIERCE AMBITION

1. WR, 3–10, 662.
2. WR, 17, 720.
3. F, 1:158–60.
4. GW, 28:203.
5. GW, 28:83.
6. GW, 1:129.
7. GW, 11:457, 1:17.
8. GW, 30:247.
9. FL, 1:108.
10. GW, 1:159.
11. GW, 1:162, 2:173.
12. FG, 44.
13. GW, 3:359.
14. GW, 2:337, 33:501; PWJA, 383.
15. F, 2:320; FL, 1:227.
16. GW, 2:437, 2:446, 32:66.
17. GW, 2:459, 469.
18. GW, 27:489; JMS, 1:359.
19. FL, 1:249.
20. F, 143–44; WR, 117.
21. GW, 2:500–501.
22. GW, 2:501.
23. GW, 37:494; F, 3:157.
24. GW, 3:84.

2: THE EDUCATION
   OF A SOLDIER

1. GW, 3:233.
2. F, 3:350–54.
3. GW, 3:232–33, 245, 229, 224.
4. GW, 3:242, 292; F, 3:404.
5. GW, 3:234; JF, 1:12.
6. JNR, 45.
7. GW, 3:240, 288.
8. JNR, 66.
9. GW, 3:277.
10. F, 3:426.
11. FL, 1:343.
12. GW, 3:293–94, 359–60.
13. GW, 4:455; WR, 184.

3: "RADICAL CURES"

1. DGW, 4:135, 167.
2. GW, 28:503.
3. VL, 14.
4. GW, 29:126.
5. GW, 29:191
6. GW, 27:481.
7. GW, 27:49, 10:5, 13:464, 19:132, 13:466.
8. WR, 518–19.
9. GW, 28:502, 29:34.
10. GW, 27:306, 28:233–34, 503, 29:169.
11. JNR, 389–90.

12. GW, 29:128; PJM, 9:378.
13. GW, 29:171.
14. WR, 635, 642, 651–52, 671.
15. DA, 21.
16. WD, 5:159.
17. RFC, 1:3–4.
18. GW, 29:192.
19. AJL, 1:196; PG, 3.
20. WC, 107.
21. RFC, 2:74.
22. VL, 37–38; PJM, 9:385.
23. RFC, 1:113, 2:541.
24. RFC, 1:254, 2:52.
25. RFC, 1:292, 295.
26. RFC, 2:30–52, 119.
27. GW, 29:245–46; RFC, 4:229.
28. RFC, 2:644.
29. RFC, 2:586–87.
30. JMS, 1:497.
31. RFC, 3:302; HS, 5:201–2, 4:275–77.
32. DGW, 5:185
33. GW, 29:358, 409.
34. GW, 28:336; RFC, 2:644.

4: THE GRAND
   EXPERIMENT BEGINS

1. VL, 66.
2. WAC, 194.

3. WR, 518–19, 710; WJA, 9:541.
4. GW, 32:47, 29:411, 26:485.
5. GW, 30:73.
6. GW, 30:395 note, 30:169, 37:573.
7. WR, 714; GW, 32:399.
8. GW, 30:186, 29:520.
9. GW, 32:133; WR, 947
10. GW, 27:367; WRL, 503–4; FL, 1:237; WR, 971.
11. GW, 30:360, 29:229; WR, 517; GW, 30:175; GM, 2:492.
12. GW, 30:255; HS, 5:335–37.
13. WR, 705; GW, 30:361.
14. WR, 468–69; JF, 1:160, 166; FL, 1:270.
15. JF, 9:449–50.
16. GW, 31:154, 30:498, 362.
17. PWJA, 392.
18. GW, 30:362 note; WJA, 9:540; FL, 3:183; WJM, 9:479; PJM, 12:155; F, 6:247.
19. DGW, 5:484 note.
20. WC, 172; FL, 3:419.
21. DGW, 5:470–85.
22. GW, 31:328; DGW, 6:132; GW, 31:318–19.
23. MAS, 88; WAC, 194; GW, 31:416.

5: THE TRANSFORMATION

1. GW, 32:116, 31:403.
2. GW, 31:173, 34:336.
3. GW, 35:138, 31:370, 32:145.
4. EM, 34.
5. JMS, 2:618; GW, 30:311.
6. GW, 31:9, 33:422, 35:228.
7. GW, 33:108, 126, 117, 122.
8. WAC, 142.
9. PJM, 12:236; LDW, 24.
10. GW, 30:305; LDW, 196.
11. HS, 11:442; JF, 1:174; HS, 18:379.
12. GW, 30:510; JF, 5:141.
13. JF, 5:148, 303.
14. GW, 31:451; JF, 1:227; LDW, 147; HS, 22:41–42, 38, 62–63.
15. JF, 1:263; LDW, 169.
16. PJM, 12:120.
17. GW, 30:415, 32:49, 31:479; HS, 19:513.
18. WJA, 1:460.
19. GW, 34:253, 30:288.
20. LDW, 32; GW, 33:403, 31:69, 32:336, 31:161.
21. GPC, 273.
22. GW, 33:320–21; FL, 3:355; GW, 30:366; EM, 55.
23. GW, 34:349; HS, 19:397,
24. GW, 31:462, 35:159.

6: THE DEEPENING
CHASM

1. HS, 16:136, 1:390.
2. GW, 31:493, 24, 30:304.
3. HS, 2:635; GW, 31:30.
4. GW, 31:52; HS, 7:149.
5. FL, 3:323.
6. PJM, 13:381.
7. VL, 88.
8. PTJ, 22:74; JMS, 2:695, 706; GW, 31:329.
9. JF, 1:200; GW, 33:488, 31:168, 319.
10. HS, 10:253.
11. HS, 3:76, 10:296.
12. GW, 31:45, 28:520, 35:315.
13. GW, 35:315.
14. PG, 16–17.
15. LDW, 58; PG, 11; LDW, 70.
16. RFC, 1:466–67.
17. HS, 19:53–57, 18:499; TDA, bk. 2, pt. 4, ch. 4.
18. GW, 33:166, 35:30–31, 32:428.
19. PJM, 14:207–8, 13:373.
20. HS, 11:559; FA, 1:118.
21. JF, 6:3.
22. JF, 1:199.
23. JF, 9:273, 307.
24. GW, 32:130–31.
25. GW, 32:132–34, 137.
26. JF, 6:101–9, 5.
27. HS, 12:347–49.
28. GW, 32:185–86.
29. PJM, 14:299–303.
30. JF, 6:5; HS, 12:137–38
31. GW, 32:310; JF, 1:216.
32. PJM, 16:215.

7: THE WIDER WORLD

1. GW, 30:305.
2. GW, 30:307.
3. GW, 4:99, 31:128, 198, 34:100.
4. RL, 154–55.
5. GW, 31:369, 32:104.
6. VL, 96–97.
7. GW, 32:39, 35:301, 31:398, 35:193–96.
8. HS, 22:553; GW, 33:465, 32:161.
9. GW, 34:30.
10. GW, 34:62.
11. JF, 7:17; GW, 34:98–99.
12. PJM, 15:406.
13. GW, 28:460, 30:487
14. HS, 16:259–60.
15. MG, 25; HS, 16:260 note.
16. WR, 329; GW, 35:57.
17. GW, 35:235–36, 359, 31:82–83; JF, 1:212, 227, 6:155.
18. GW, 32:447–48; JMS, 2:770.

19. GW, 32:390, 469, 447–48.
20. SIP, 19; PJM, 15:83.
21. GW, 33:164.
22. JMS, 2:787; F, 7:87.
23. HS, 14:403, 407; GW, 32:39.
24. GW, 30:186, 33:484–85.
25. HS, 5:483, 19:69–70; JF, 1:206.
26. EM, 421–23; JMS, 2:905.
27. F, 7:283 note.
28. GW, 34:244.
29. GW, 34:293, 295, 398–403, 413; F, 7:338.
30. JF, 7:40; GW, 35:30, 32; FA, 1:188; HS, 25:457.
31. FA, 1:196.
32. EM, 439, 376.
33. GW, 34:315.
34. VL, 105.

8: THE CURTAIN FALLS

1. GW, 35:141–42 note, 34:147–48.
2. GW, 35:199–200.
3. GW, 35:230, 31:30.
4. GW, 29:171, 35:37.
5. GW, 34:251, 266.
6. GW, 34:320; SR, 108.
7. GW, 33:23, 96, 31:477–78, 32:200, 35:174, 34:262–63.
8. GW, 35:409.
9. GW, 33:506.
10. GW, 33:476, 506, 523.
11. JF, 1:253.
12. PJM, 15:406–7.
13. GW, 34:280, 33:476.
14. GW, 34:251, 262–64, 35:358.
15. WR, 952, 946, GW, 25:359; F, 7:320; JF, 1:254.
16. JF, 7:101–2.
17. TDA, bk. 1, pt. 2, ch. 2.
18. GW, 35:91.
19. GW, 35:138, 146.
20. GW, 35:102, 123–24 note; EM, 502, 538.
21. GW, 35:142–43 note.
22. GW, 35:99; WR, 941–42.
23. GW, 29:479; JF, 8:339.
24. GW, 35:178 note, 205.
25. GW, 34:264.
26. GW, 34:407.
27. JF, 5:76.
28. GW, 35:409.
29. JAW, 2:245, 247; JMS, 2:955.
30. GW, 35:430; WR, 1003–4.
31. GF, 10:476; GW, 37:23, 76, 327.
32. GF, 14:31.
33. GW, 37:132, 312–13.
34. GF, 14:119–20.
35. HS, 21:467; GF, 14:6–7, 123–24.
36. GW, 37:428–29.

9: COLLECTIVE
  LEADERSHIP:
  REMAKING THE
  CONSTITUTION

1. FB, 14.
2. SL, 109.
3. FB, 137–38.
4. WAC, 168.
5. WBC, 103.
6. LLF, passim.
7. *New York Times,* 14 January
   2003.

8. PG, 29.
9. PG, 30–31.
10. WLC, 179.

EPILOGUE:
MORAL LEADERSHIP:
THE MIXED LEGACY

1. FG, 73, 331, 398, 486.
2. GW, 29:5; WAS.
3. GW, 31:29–30.

Milestones

1732 Born in Bridges Creek, Westmoreland County, Virginia, February 22.

1754–58 Serves as lieutenant colonel in French and Indian Wars.

1759 Marries Martha Dandridge Custis.
Elected to House of Burgesses; will serve as a burgess until 1775.

1761 Inherits Mount Vernon estate.

1774 Chosen delegate to First Continental Congress.

1775 Elected commander in chief of Continental Army at Second Continental Congress.

1781 Defeats British troops at Yorktown.

1783 Retires to Mount Vernon.

1787 Elected president of the Constitutional Convention in Philadelphia.

1789 Unanimously elected president of the United States.
Appoints heads of executive departments of state, treasury, war; sets up executive branch of government.

1791 Signs bill chartering the Bank of the United States.
Selects site for new capital city on the Potomac River.

1792 Unanimously reelected to a second presidential term.
Tries to mediate feud between Jefferson and Hamilton.

1793 Proclaims American neutrality after France declares war on Great Britain, Spain, and the Netherlands.

1794 Leads troops to put down Whiskey Rebellion in western Pennsylvania.

1795 Signs Jay's Treaty, a commercial treaty with Great Britain. Signs the Treaty of San Lorenzo with Spain, giving Americans access to the Mississippi River.

1796 Publishes his Farewell Address.

1798 Leaves retirement to accept post as commander in chief of army.

1799 Dies December 14.
       Leaves instructions to free his slaves upon his death, or upon Martha's death, should she outlive him.

Acknowledgments

We are grateful to Milton Djuric for his indispensable contributions, to Joseph Ellis for reviewing our manuscript, and to Robert and Lee Dalzell for sharing their enthusiasm for Washington with us. Alison O'Grady, Walter Komorowski, and Rebecca Ohm at the Williams College Library, Donna Chenail and her colleagues in the Faculty Secretarial Office, and Alan Hirsch all assisted us in various ways.

Index

ABOUT THE AUTHORS

James MacGregor Burns is the Woodrow Wilson Professor of Government Emeritus at Williams College and a senior scholar at the Jepson School of Leadership Studies at the University of Richmond. He is the author of numerous books, including *Transforming Leadership: A New Pursuit of Happiness*, *Roosevelt: The Lion and the Fox*, and the Pulitzer Prize–winning *Roosevelt: The Soldier of Freedom*. He is a past president of the American Political Science Association.

Susan Dunn is Professor of Humanities at Williams College. She is the author of many books, including *Sister Revolutions: French Lightning, American Light*, *The Deaths of Louis XVI*, and *The Three Roosevelts: Patrician Leaders Who Transformed America* (with James MacGregor Burns). Burns and Dunn live in Williamstown, Massachusetts.